SQUADRONS!

No. 25

THE SUPERMARINE

SPITFIRE MK. V

- THE EAGLE SQUADRONS -

PHIL H. LISTEMANN

ISBN: 979-1096490-22-6

Copyright

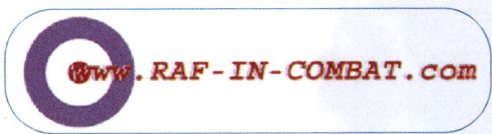

Colour profiles: Gaetan Marie/Bravo Bravo Aviation

PERSONEL :

(AUS)/RAF: Australian serving in the RAF
(BEL)/RAF: Belgian serving in the RAF
(CAN)/RAF: Canadian serving in the RAF
(CZ)/RAF: Czechoslovak serving in the RAF
(NFL)/RAF: Newfoundlander serving in the RAF
(NL)/RAF: Dutch serving in the RAF
(NZ)/RAF: New Zealander serving in the RAF
(POL)/RAF: Pole serving in the RAF
(RHO)/RAF: Rhodesian serving in the RAF
(SA)/RAF: South African serving in the RAF
(US)/RAF - RCAF : American serving in the RAF or RCAF

OTHER

ATA: Air Transport Auxiliary
CO : Commander
DFC : Distinguished Flying Cross
DFM : Distinguished Flying Medal
DSO : Distinguished Service Order
Eva. : Evaded
ORB : Operational Record Book
OTU : Operational Training Unit
PoW : Prisoner of War
PAF: Polish Air Force
RAF : Royal Air Force
RAAF : Royal Australian Air Force
RCAF : Royal Canadian Air Force
RNZAF : Royal New Zealand Air Force
SAAF : South African Air Force
s/d: Shot down
Sqn : Squadron
† : Killed

RANKS

G/C : Group Captain
W/C : Wing Commander
S/L : Squadron Leader
F/L : Flight Lieutenant
F/O : Flying Officer
P/O : Pilot Officer
W/O : Warrant Officer
F/Sgt : Flight Sergeant
Sgt : Sergeant
Cpl : Corporal
LAC : Leading Aircraftman

CODENAMES - OFFENSIVE OPERATIONS - FIGHTER COMMAND

CIRCUS:
Bombers heavily escorted by fighters, the purpose being to bring enemy fighters into combat.

RAMROD:
Bombers escorted by fighters, the primary aim being to destroy a target.

RANGER:
Large formation freelance intrusion over enemy territory with aim of wearing down enemy figthers.

RHUBARD:
Freelance fighter sortie against targets of opportunity.

ROADSTEAD:
Dive bombing and low level attacks on enemy ships at sea or in harbour

RODEO:
A fighter sweep without bombers.

SWEEP:
An offensive flight by fighters designed to draw up and clear the enemy from the sky.

THE SUPERMARINE SPITFIRE MK V

Paradoxically, the Mk.V, which ended up being the most numerous variant of the famous fighter built, was not even an intended development of the design. Indeed, it was only considered because of the abandonment of the Spitfire Mk.III. As the Luftwaffe was continually improving its formidable Messerschmitt Bf 109, the latest version of which, the Bf 109F, clearly outclassed the Spitfire Mk.II, the British had no other option but to rapidly find a successor to the latter. At this time, at the end of 1940, the British did not know what the Germans' were planning and expected them to carry on undertaking daylight raids upon the return of nicer weather. The RAF, therefore, wanted to be ready to counter the new German fighter developments. A solution was soon found by mounting a Merlin 45 (former Merlin III), a simplified version of the Merlin XX, on a slightly strengthened Spitfire Mk.I or Mk.II airframe. Several Spitfires were thus modified, with either a Merlin 45 or Merlin 46, during the first weeks of 1941. The resulting feedback was good and the Air Ministry requested that Supermarine modify, as early as possible, Spitfires already on the assembly lines so they could be put into service as rapidly as possible. This is how the Spitfire Mk.V (Supermarine's Type 349) came to be.

It entered service during spring 1941 and the first Fighter Command units to receive them were Nos. 41, 54, 64, 91 and 92 Squadrons. The converted aircraft soon gave way to aircraft that began their lives in the factory as Mk.Vs. The new mark was built in three main variants until October 1943 and the last example, EF753, was delivered to the RAF the following month. Only 94 Spitfire Mk.VAs were constructed because its eight 0.303 machine-guns were no longer the ideal armament composition for modern combat. While few of this version were built, approximately 125 Mk.Is/IIs were modified in 1941 and 1942 to swell the ranks of units equipped with the Mk.VA. The Spitfire Mk.VB was a Mk.VA armed with two 20mm cannon and four .303 machine guns, a combination that became the standard Spitfire armament. In all, 3923 of this variant were built and it became the standard RAF fighter of 1941 and 1942, putting the Hurricane into the background within Fighter Command. The Spitfire Mk.VC which followed was a further developed variant and was equipped with the new, so-called 'universal' wing that allowed for the mounting of four 20mm cannon, or two cannons (with the capacity to carry double the amount of rounds) and four 0.303 machine-guns. With 2447 built, this was the main variant that was sent overseas and which formed the backbone of units fighting over Malta, in North Africa, and, later, in the Far East (see SQUADRONS! 3). In all, 6464 Mk.Vs were delivered to the RAF (plus almost 200 conversions).

The Mk.V fought on all fronts, but it was also widely exported with first deliveries to foreign countries beginning during the war. The British leased hundreds of Mk.Vs to the Americans for their fighter groups in Europe and the Mediterranean, and many also went to Australia, the Soviet Union and the Free French. The RAF, however, remained the main user and no less than 150 RAF fighter squadrons were equipped with the Mk.V between 1941 and 1945. It saw heavy fighting in 1941 and 1942 and also suffered heavy losses. By 1 January 1945, the RAF had no more than 1500 examples left, less than a quarter of what had been manufactured or converted. However, the Mk.V had accounted for approximately 1000 kills in Western Europe, 800 over Malta and North Africa, roughly 300 in the Mediterranean (two thirds of which were attributed to American fighter groups), thirty in the Far East and around seventy by aircraft operating from Australia. This longevity can also be explained by the fact that the Mk.V had managed to evolve and adapt to

A line of Spitfire Mk.Vs in spring 1941. W3127, in the foreground, was part of a contract for 450 Spitfire Mk.Is signed in March 1940 (W3109-W3970) that was soon amended to Mk.Vs before the first aircraft had left the factory. W3127 was delivered in April 1941 and was not removed from the RAF inventory until December 1946.

The man who started it all, Colonel Sweeny, right, in RAF uniform. He served with the French Foreign Legion in early W.W.I and soon found himself in charge of its small American unit. In 1915 he was commissioned in the Legion, the first American to be so promoted. He was wounded the same year and was also the first American to be awarded the Legion of Honour. When the USA entered the war, he joined the US Army and ended the war as a lieutenant-colonel. He continued his career as a soldier of fortune post- war and, logically, when France was at war once more in 1939, he wished to help build a new Lafayette *escadrille*. France collapsed before the project came to fruition, but the RAF would inherit the project.

new theatres of operations where the RAF was operating. Indeed, from 1943 onwards, with the progressive introduction of the Mk.IX, many would be re-equipped with engines that performed better at low altitude (particularly the Merlin 50M and 55M) and often with clipped wings to improve handling at these altitudes. Thus modified, the Mk.V was able to remain on the front-line until 1945 when a variant optimised for low altitudes, the Mk. XVI, was at last available in sufficient numbers.

The Spitfire Mk.V did not survive for long once the war was over, however. The Mk.VA was declassed in September 1945, the Mk.VBs and VCs were very quickly scrapped, and the last aircraft were removed from inventories in March 1948.

RECRUTING AMERICAN PILOTS

From the very beginning of the war in Europe, Americans, at all levels, took an interest in the conflict realising that, sooner or later, they would be involved. Creating a fighter squadron comprising American volunteers quickly took root in certain minds, including Charles Sweeny's, an ex-serviceman of the French Foreign Legion during the Great War. He had been inspired by the exploits of the famous American-manned Lafayette squadron, and the status it held, all of which had been portrayed by the media of the time. He established a network, allowing interested Americans to cross the Atlantic to support France, although French enthusiasm on this occasion was not so positive. Compounding Sweeny's problems was a Congress Neutrality Act, voted in 1935 and revised and reinforced many times thereafter, making the recruiting of American volunteers for fighting in foreign countries very difficult indeed. The US authorities closely monitored activity of this nature and would not facilitate any enlistment. Volunteers or, for that matter, anyone suspected of being one, would be detained at the Canadian border. This situation remained right up until the fall of France in June 1940. As a result, volunteers arrived too late and the French, overwhelmed by their own situation, had little to offer them. Consequently, the vast majority disappeared amid the upheaval, either killed or made prisoners, while others returned to the USA by their own means. Only five of the original volunteers are known to have arrived in Great Britain.

Thereafter the situation changed and American authorities became more accommodating. At the same time the number of volunteers increased, since many were aware that the USA was preparing to enter the war. The Knight Committee, named for its founder, was set up and this organisation would be responsible for the bulk of American recruitment from the spring of 1940. In August 1941 this committee became the Canadian Aviation Bureau before it was disbanded in late 1942. Some 250 American pilots would serve with three American fighter units - the Eagle Squadrons - formed within the RAF between 1940 and 1942. These men, though, were only a fraction of the hundreds who passed through the committee to enrol in the RAF, or the RCAF, and fight under the RAF umbrella in Europe, the Middle East and the Far East. Their motives were varied, but the majority simply sought adventure. Their aspirations were to become pilots, but many had been refused entry into their own country's air arms on educational, competency or medical grounds (or a combination of those). Both the RCAF and the RAF (Royal Air Force Volunteer Reserve - RAFVR) provided viable alternatives and the prospect of flying a Spitfire, by then the best Allied fighter, only strengthened their desire to join up. The American pilots, in particular those that served with the Eagle Squadrons, were to benefit from certain privileges. Most were not required to pledge allegiance to the King upon their engagement and thus were able to maintain their American citizenship. Additionally, it was understood that, those passed by the Knight Committee would be commissioned at the end of their training, as opposed to the majority of those who joined the RCAF and graduated as Non-Commissioned Officers. This disparity was to create problems when the integration of these pilots into the USAAF took place.

TRANSFER TO THE AAF

The transfer of personnel to the AAF, a natural outcome, was not so simple for numerous reasons. Firstly, the RAF had put a considerable investment into their training, and they were fully operational, and doing a fine job, when America entered the war in December 1941. The British simply were not in a hurry to disband the three American fighter squadrons. The pilots themselves had signed up with the RAFVR until the end of the war and, adding to English woes, they now faced war on a new front with Japan. Integration into the AAF meant that the pilots trained by the RAF would, sooner or later, come into contact with countrymen trained in American schools and this would not be to everyone's satisfaction. At certain levels 'Eagle' flyers had been subjected to a British influence, not always well embraced by Americans.

Rank equivalence also posed problems. The AAF did not have anyone below the base rank of second lieutenant as a pilot . NCOs transferring from the RCAF would automatically have to become second lieutenants. The situation involving officers was relatively straightforward - they would transfer to the comparative rank. There was also debate about how these transferees should be utilised. Eighth Air Force officials of rank felt that it would be logical to divide these pilots among AAF units arriving in England where their solid experience would be of some benefit.

Others were of the opinion that the three Eagle squadrons, having established a fine reputation and not wishing to separate, should be forged into a specific unit - the 4th Fighter Group (FG). In effect this was what happened in September 1942. However, some pilots chose to remain with the RAF out of loyalty and feeling a transfer would not be in their best interests.

As for the 4th FG, it was to keep its unique identity for the early months of its existence, but, by the summer of 1943, due to losses and turnover, it would become an American Fighter Group, falling in line with all of the others.

For those who chose to integrate into the AAF, it was not immediately apparent whether they had made the correct choice or not. While they gained a pay increase and access to an array of typically American luxuries, they lost an element of prestige with the British population who held them in high regard - they were considered to be a cut above the average American. There was also the loss of spirit and friendship, very present within the British units, which became more obvious with the arrival of American pilots coming from the USA to replace those who were lost or had left.

The pilots of the Eagle Squadrons were special, being volunteers in a British war that was not theirs and, for political reasons, they had been courted by and received a great deal of press. Once integration into the AAF had taken place, this became something of a burden. The AAF moved quickly to tone down their amount of press coverage, so that they would become less conspicuous, for both morale and political reasons.

The end of an era. The three RAF fighter squadrons are transferred to the USAAF in a ceremony on 29 September 1942. Here Air Chief Marshal Sir Sholto Douglas, Commander-in-Chief RAF Fighter Command, is reviewing the Eagle pilots. The three Eagle squadrons had been brought together on the same base a short time earlier, having fought separately since their respective formations. Note the pilots are wearing their RAF uniforms, but all already been officially transferred to the USAAF and were no longer members of the RAF.

Victories - confirmed or probable claims: 39.0

First operational sortie:
01.09.41

Last operational sortie:
27.09.42

Number of sorties: 3,271

Total aircraft written-off: 27

Aircraft lost on operations: 21
Aircraft lost in accidents: 6

Squadron code letters:
XR

COMMANDING OFFICERS

S/L Stanley T. Meares (†)	RAF No. 37683	RAF	...	15.11.41
S/L Chesley G. Peterson	RAF No. 83706	(US)/RAF	17.11.41	27.08.42
S/L Gregory A. Daymond	RAF No. 84657	(US)/RAF	27.08.42	...

SQUADRON USAGE

The first Eagle squadron to be formed, initially flying Hurricanes, this unit was also the first to make the transition to the Spitfire. The Mk.IIs arrived in August 1941. The squadron was part of the North Weald Wing at the time and had been commanded by a

British officer, Squadron Leader S.T. Meares, since 24 August. He had previously been the OC of No. 74 Squadron. The first Spitfire Vs (W3509, W3627, AB783, AB810-11, AB875, AB900, AB907, AB815 and AD123) arrived just before the end of August and the first operations were flown alongside Spitfire IIs. There was no need to waste time converting to the Mk.V as the two types were very similar. The full complement of Spitfire Vs had been received by early September and it cannot be said that the introduction of the Mk.V did not get off to a good start for the squadron. While only two confirmed victories had been claimed with the Spitfire IIs in over a month, the unit claimed two Bf109s destroyed, another probable and one damaged during a bomber escort to Mazingarbe on the 4th. The victorious pilots were P/O G.A. Daymond from Montana, P/O T.C. Wallace from Pennsylvania, P/O R.L. Mannix from New York, and P/O M.W. Fessler from Wisconsin. Those claims were made for no loss so it really was a good start. Three days later, the squadron, led by the CO, took part in a sweep to St-Omer in the north of France. The Luftwaffe did not make it easy for them. While F/L Chesley Peterson, the American B Flight commander from Idaho, managed to shoot down a Bf109, the engagement was not one-sided and three pilots were posted missing. Pilot Officers H.S. Fenlow from Texas and E.Q. Tobin from Utah were both later declared killed in action. Eugene Tobin was a great loss for the squadron as he was a founding member of the unit and had fought in the Battle of Britain with No. 609 Squadron. The third pilot missing, P/O W.H. Nichols from California, was captu-

Stanley Meares was a pre-war RAF officer and started the war as a fighter pilot with 74 Sqn. At the end of 1939 he was posted to HQ Fighter Command and was the senior controller at Hornchurch throughout the Battle of Britain. He returned to flying duties in May 1941, joining 611 Sqn as a flight commander, before he was given command of his pre-war unit at the end of June. He was awarded the DFC in July and joined 71 Sqn in August as OC.

Two prominent American faces of 71 Sqn during the Spitfire era. Left, 'Gus' Daymond and, right, 'Pete' Peterson. The photo was taken when both were awarded the DFC, the first Eagles to receive the award. At the time, Peterson was a flight commander and was to become the only Eagle pilot to receive the DSO when he was awarded it in September 1942.

red and was sent to a PoW camp. A fourth Spitfire, flown by Texan P/O F.P. Dowling, was seriously damaged by the Bf109s and had to make a forced landing near the airfield. While Dowling escaped injury, his aircraft was only good for scrap. Over the next few days, 71 was involved in convoy or dawn patrols until the 16th when another sweep over France was carried out. It proved uneventful, but was followed by an escort of 24 Blenheims attacking Mazingarbe the next day (*Circus* 95). The Bf109s soon interfered over Dunkirk and Pilot Officers T.P. McGerty (Texas) and New Yorker W.D. Geiger were soon separated from the rest of the formation. McGerty was shot down and killed by the Bf109s and Geiger, with three Bf109s after him, barely avoided the same fate. Hit, he was able to bale out and land in the English Channel. After floating for about five hours, he was rescued by a German patrol boat and spent the rest of the war in captivity. Despite these two losses, another bomber escort was organised later in the evening, but this time everyone made it back to base. The squadron would get its revenge the following day when F/L Peterson claimed a Bf109 destroyed and another damaged south of Le Touquet during the first op of the day (another bomber escort). The following day, P/O G.A. Daymond, accompanied by J. Flynn from Illinois, flew a *Rhubarb* over the Continent. They encountered some Bf109s and fared well with the American pilots returning with one confirmed Bf109 each, Daymond damaging another. The second op, a naval escort, was uneventful. Bomber escort was the task given to the Wing on the 20th, the 21st and then again on the 27th. On the second of those, the Americans fought against the Bf109s once more and some pilots returned victorious. 'Red' McColpin, from New York State and recently posted from No. 121 Squadron, was successful, while P/O C.W. Tribken, also from New York State, claimed a probable. It was during the operation of the 27th (*Circus* 103), however, that the unit would make its best claims with two Bf109s destroyed, three more claimed as probables, and one damaged. The claims were shared between F/L Peterson, P/O Sam Mauriello (New York City), who opened his score after nine months of operations with the squadron, Californian P/O J.G. DuFour (but using the identity of J.J. Crowley) and R.O. Scarborough from New Mexico. Scarborough was a newcomer from No. 133 Squadron and, like DuFour and Mauriello, opened his score during this op. The damaged aircraft was claimed by O.H. Coen from North Dakota. September ended with an uneventful *Rhubarb*. The month had been a very successful and intensive one, despite the relatively small number of operations flown, 200 for the Spitfire V, compared to more than 400 in August. The introduction of the Mk.V, despite the early losses, showed promise for the squadron.

While September can be regarded as an intense month of operations, October, despite the 250 sorties flown, was almost routine. An uneventful fighter sweep was flown on the first day of the month to kick things off. The next day, 71 participated in a bomber escort to Abbeville. Intercepted by Bf109s, the squadron managed to shoot down five of them, including one for the CO, in the ensuing melee. The other four were credited to American pilots. McColpin, who was to become one of the unit's most successful pilots, shot down two, while P/O Scarborough shared a claim with P/O N. Anderson from Louisiana who opened his score in this occasion. The other claim went to another pilot who also opened his score – 'Art' Roscoe from Illinois. This tally was obtained for no loss. The following day, a bomber escort to Nieuport and a *Rhubarb* with three aircraft were flown, but no enemy aircraft were encountered. During the next six days there was no operational flying, but F/L Chesley Peterson and F/O 'Gus' Daymond were awarded the DFC on the 4th. They were the first Eagle pilots to receive this honour. On the 10th and 11th, operational flying resumed quietly with four Spitfires flying a *Rhubarb* each day and a handful of convoy patrols being dutifully carried out. On 12 October, among other operational sorties, the squadron participated in a bomber escort to Boulogne, followed by another one the next day to Mazingarbe. Twelve aircraft took off at 13.25 with the CO leading. The Luftwaffe soon made its appearance. At the end of the combat, P/O G.C. Daniel (RCAF) was missing. He was later reported as a PoW at Stalag Luft III, having drifted in his dinghy for more than seventy hours before being washed up on the shores of France suffering a fractured knee and frostbite. He was an interesting man as he was a Native American from Oklahoma and had previously served with Nos. 121 (Eagle) and 133 (Eagle) Squadrons before being posted to 71 in September. He was to be one of the few pilots to serve in all three of the Eagle squadrons. It was a period of bad luck for 71 Squadron as, two days later, Texan P/O R.A. Atkinson was killed. While doing aerobatics, a wing collapsed in level flight. Even though he baled out of his stricken aircraft, he was too low for his parachute to deploy properly and was killed when he hit the ground. Having arrived the previous month, he was about to be declared operational. One week later, the squadron lost another pilot in an accident. Pilot Officer L.A. Chatterton, from Brooklyn, also lost a wing while turning steeply. He had only begun his operational experience earlier in the month. In the meantime, operations continued and, on the 16th, the squadron was able to avenge the loss of Daniel, shot down three days previously, when, during a *Rhubarb*, McColpin managed to shoot down a Hs126. Four days later, P/O Coen took off at 06.30 with F/L 'Pete' Peterson on a *Rhubarb*. They found a train and strafed it, but Coen's Spitfire was damaged, when the train exploded, and he had to bale out. Luckily, he was not captured and, with the help of the French underground, he evaded capture and was back with the squadron at the end of December. Pilot Officer M.W. Fessler of Wisconsin had a similar experience when his Spitfire was also damaged by an exploding train on the 27th. He was not as lucky as Coen, however, and saw out the war as a PoW. On the credit side, P/O Scarborough claimed a Bf109 on the 25th while on a *Rhubarb* and McColpin made a double claim on the 27th, which took him to ace status, during the same op when Fessler was shot down.

In November, the squadron flew more than 200 sorties, a good figure considering the unit could not fly for almost half of the month. The main reason was the weather which began to deteriorate as the month progressed. Most of the sorties carried out were convoy patrols with only a handful of ops flown over the Continent. On the 1st, the squadron participated in an escort of Hurricanes and bombers to Hardelot, an op that was repeated on the 4th. Three days later, a *Rhubarb*, led by the CO, was flown during which P/O T.C. Wallace (Pennsylvania) claimed a Bf109 destroyed over the Dunkirk area. The next day, 71 flew a *Circus* and the last offensi-

The third Eagle pilot to receive the DFC was 'Red' McColpin, seen here congratulated by his squadron mates in November 1941 in front of his Spitfire (AB908/XR-Y) with four swastikas painted under the cockpit. McColpin also served with Nos. 121 and 133 Sqns, making him one of the very few American pilots to have served with all three of the Eagle units.

The most claims made by 71 Sqn were made while operating the Spitfire V. However, it also suffered most of its losses, including AA855/XR-C in which P/O M.W. Fessler was shot down to become a PoW on 27 October 1941. *(Andrew Thomas)*

ve sorties of the month were flown on the 27th when Hurricanes and bombers were escorted to Boulogne. This raid was led by the new CO, C.G. Peterson, who took over the squadron following the death of S/L Meares on the 15th when he collided with P/O R.O. Scarborough during a practice flight. Scarborough was also killed in the collision. Peterson had climbed to this position in a year after having joined the squadron as a pilot officer in November 1940. He was the first Eagle pilot to lead a RAF fighter squadron. He was replaced at the head of B Flight by P/O N. Anderson and, as P/O Daymond had taken over A Flight at the beginning of the month, the squadron was now entirely led by Americans from an operational point of view. December proved rather uneventful with about 150 sorties flown. A move to Martlesham Heath changed things up a bit, but got off to a good start when P/O E.M. Potter, from Minnesota, shared in a damaged Ju88 off Orford Ness with a pilot from No. 19 Squadron during a convoy patrol on 27th. The squadron had moved to its new station on the 14th and remained there for the next four and a half months.

In January, the squadron was involved in convoy patrols, with a couple of *Rhubarbs* and scrambles flown to break the routine. While not very intense for the American pilots, they flew close to 400 sorties despite the last week of January being washed out by bad weather. The squadron did make its mark during the month, however. During one of the few *Rhubarbs*, on the 9th, Pilot Officers E.M. Potter and R.S. Sprague (Washington State), the only participants on this op, each claimed one Fw190 destroyed three miles off Le Tréport. They were both newcomers who had only been with the squadron since the middle of autumn. Two days later, in the morning, F/O 'Sam' Mauriello and Californian P/O L.S. Nomis scrambled to 8000 feet to intercept a lone enemy aircraft. Several vectors were given by the Controller and the section became separated in cloud. After receiving further vectors, Nomis found himself well out to sea and, flying at 12,000 feet, turned for home. He saw a Ju88 breaking through a 10/10ths cloud layer at 11,000 feet and about 600 yards to his right. He immediately attacked it from the beam to the right quarter with a two second burst. Nomis saw pieces falling off the right wing of the Junkers. Then he directed his fire towards the cockpit of the Ju88 and saw some of his bullets striking home. Almost immediately the enemy aircraft dived into cloud cover and was not seen again. On returning to the base, Nomis claimed the aircraft as damaged. The bad weather at the end of January made the aerodrome unserviceable until 16 February. After three weeks of inactivity, 71 was ordered to scramble at 11.30 to intercept an enemy aircraft. Flying Officer C.L. Martin, from Pennsylvania, saw a Do217, but lost it almost immediately in cloud. Less than one hour later, another section took off on another scramble, but was recalled after ten minutes. A base patrol was followed by further scrambles, but nothing happened until the middle of the afternoon when Green Section, Pilot Officers Coen and H.L. Stewart (from North Carolina), saw a Do217 attempting to attack a convoy. The two American pilots attacked at once and fired all of their ammunition. The Dornier was hit and the Americans saw the aircraft entering cloud with black smoke pouring from it. Soon after they saw another Dornier that found cloud cover before they could make an attack. Green Section then returned to base where Coen filed a combat report for a damaged Do217. Uneventful convoy patrols were carried out the next day and, on the 24th, P/O J.J. Lynch from Ohio and P/O H.F. Marting from Indiana flew a Rhubarb over France where they strafed some ground targets, soldiers and a train, but no enemy aircraft were encountered. Lynch brought back a piece of telegraph pole in his wing proving that he flew very, very low! At the end of the month, F/L Daymond, on long leave, was replaced at the head of A Flight by Sam Mauriello. Despite two weeks of inactivity, the squadron flew 230 sorties in February. In March, it completed close to 300 sorties, but the pilots had to wait until the 26th to break the monotony of the convoy patrols they were flying. That day, Black Section (Pilot Officers F.P. Dowling and Canadian-born American W.T. O'Regan) scrambled to patrol at 5000 feet. They soon spotted a lone enemy aircraft and Dowling fired two bursts, but observed nothing. The section was recalled immediately as there was doubt as to the identity of the aircraft. The month ended with a *Rhubarb* flown by F/L Anderson and P/O T.J. Andrews, but they returned to base with nothing to report.

In April, with spring and its favourable weather, activity increased steadily and, with more than 600 sorties flown, the squadron was more than adequately employed! In the first nine days, operational activity consisted of convoy patrols or scrambles and the pilots had to wait until the 10th to operate over the Continent when an uneventful *Rodeo* was flown. Two days later, a *Circus* went to Hazebrouck where the Luftwaffe was encountered and a quick dogfight took place. The Americans were not in a good position to make any claims and only one pilot was able to get a single burst in. The Germans, with the advantage, had more luck and shot down P/O B.F. Mays from Texas. The squadron flew a fighter sweep on the 14th followed by two *Circuses* on the 15th and a *Rodeo* on the 16th during which P/O O.H. Coen managed to damage a Fw190. The next morning, 71 returned to convoy patrols and, on the first one, P/O J.J. Lynch and P/O L.S. Nomis saw a lone Ju88. They both gave a chase but, while closing in, the German rear gunner hit Lynch's Spitfire and he was obliged to break off and return to base where he crashed and was injured. During that time, Nomis continued to engage and ran out of ammunition. His final burst must have been a good one as when he pulled away he saw the bomber diving into the sea. The same day, the squadron participated in a late morning *Circus* and a *Rodeo* in the middle of the afternoon, but each time the pilots returned with nothing to report. Defensive work was the routine over the following days until the 24th when a bomber escort (*Ramrod*) was flown. This was followed by two more the next day and the day after. During the last one, P/O R. McMinn (Oklahoma) ran out of fuel and was lucky to make a crash landing at Manston on return. He escaped injury, but that was to be the last flight for his Spitfire. On the 27th, the squadron escorted Hurribombers to Saint-Omer. The Luftwaffe tried to interfere over the target, but 71 did its job of protecting the Hurricanes. Squadron Leader Peterson managed to shoot down two Fw190s, and damaged a third, while P/O Coen, and M.G. McPharlin from Illinois, claimed the destruction of three others that they shared between them. Pilot Officer 'Art' Roscoe added a probable to the tally while Pilot Officers R.S. Sprague and E.M. Potter each clamed one Fw190 damaged. On the debit side, P/O J.V. Flynn from Illinois was posted missing, victim of the Fw190s, while P/O J.A. Gray from California returned to base with such damage to his aircraft that it was declared beyond economical repair. On the 28th, the squadron escorted bombers in the middle of the morning and, in the afternoon, flew convoy patrols. The following day,

only offensive ops were flown including a Circus that, upon the squadron's return to base, saw P/O Nomis make a bad landing. The Spitfire overturned in soft ground and was wrecked. The last two days of April were also busy, with one *Circus* and two scrambles on the 29th, and then two scrambles, one *Ramrod*, and a *Circus* to Abbeville, during which two more claims for damaged Fw190s were added by S/L Peterson and F/L Mauriello.

In May, activity decreased to a little more than 200 sorties, but the squadron reached the 5000 sortie mark since its formation in November 1940. In that time it had been one of the most active Fighter Command units. The squadron was now operating from Debden. It was a low scoring month with one probable over an unidentified aircraft during a bomber escort to Hazelbrouck on the 9th claimed by P/O Coen, and a Fw190 damaged on the 19th by the CO. Aside from the convoy patrols, 71 also flew ten bomber escorts, six fighter sweeps and a *Rhubarb*.

June began with two new flight commanders, G.A. Daymond returning to the head of his flight, while Oscar Coen took over B Flight. Three claims were made on the first day of the month, one confirmed and one damaged for Peterson, one confirmed for Daymond (initially claimed as damaged), and one each damaged for Pilot Officers R.S. Sprague and E.M. Potter. Those combats took place as part of the Debden Wing (with Nos. 350 and 111 Squadrons) which

Joe M. Kelly from California (left) and Edward T. Miluck from North Dakota (right). Like many Eagle pilots, the lack of opportunities forced them to volunteer to serve overseas. Kelly and Miluck flew in Africa in 1942 before being transferred to the USAAF in December 1942 and January 1943 respectively. Neither pilot was required for combat operations again.

'Chief' Nomis on the wing of his Spitfire. Note the Indian chief painted on the aircraft. He chose this personal artwork as his father was part Sioux Indian. Nomis did not transfer at the same time as his squadron mates and was posted to Malta in August 1942. He later served in North Africa with 92 Sqn. He finally transferred to the USAAF in March 1943, but was sent Stateside. He was medically discharged in July 1944 because of wounds received while in Tunisia. After the war he flew for the Chinese Air Force, from 1950 to 1951, and the Indonesian Air Force from 1952 to 1954.

was despatched to escort eight Hurribombers. The squadron was flying middle cover at 23,000 feet, with 111 Squadron at 20,000 and the Belgians at 25,000 feet. The combat was not, however, one-sided as Californian P/O G. Teicheira failed to return. The next day, 71 was called to participate in an ASR mission, one flight relieving another in sequence. At 08.30, B Flight, led by F/L Coen, took off and, during the trip, the engine of the Spitfire flown by P/O Zavakos (Ohio) caused trouble. He was seen to crash into the sea thirty miles from Martlesham Heath. He did not survive the crash. The squadron participated in further ops over the Continent in June, but opportunities to fire at German aircraft were rare and no claim was made. The only occasion occurred on the 20th when P/O J.F. Helgason, from California, fired at a Fw190, but observed no results. July, however, was a bit special. The squadron was kept at readiness until the 8th. After that, operations were discontinued and the squadron declared non-operational prior to being posted overseas. This order was cancelled soon after. Flying activity resumed on the 15th, but only training flights were flown. Despite being at readiness during the following days, nothing happened on the operational side of things. However, luck was with Pilot Officers J.J. Lynch and J.F. Helgason on the 19th when the North Weald Wing came to Debden early in the afternoon to join the Debden Wing on a *Rhubarb*. As their unit had been released for the whole day for training duties, the two 71 Squadron pilots had, coincidentally, just taken off for a local flight. They took the opportunity to latch onto the Spitfires of No. 222 Squadron and headed to Dunkirk. Near Dunkirk, they headed towards Nieuport, the two Eagles flying in wide echelon. Lynch and Helgason then turned with the Wing to the right, through 180°, and flew back along the coast. On the turn, Lynch and Helgason were between the Wing and the coast. As they flew west along the coast, two Fw190s broke cloud in a dive, shallowing out so they approached head on. When within range Lynch fired a short burst at the Fw190 farthest from the coast. The German was already firing at someone, but the sudden appearance of Lynch made him stop. As the Fw190 passed, Lynch looked back and saw it half-rolling onto its back. Before turning he looked ahead and saw four more Fw190s just below the cloud and approaching head-on. He pulled up, firing a burst into the group which split up as it passed overhead. At the same time, Helgason also opened fire at an oncoming Fw190. Lynch then had to pull up into cloud to avoid a section of Spitfires. Helgason by this time had called that his engine was causing trouble and when Lynch broke cloud again the sky was clear. Eventually both pilots managed to return to base and could file a claim for a destroyed Fw190 shared between them as a call from Wing Commander Scott-Malden reported that he and his pilots had seen it going into the sea.

The squadron was released for daily training later in the day until the 21st when a *Rhubarb* was flown by twelve aircraft over the Blankenberge-Dunkirk area. Further fighter sweeps were carried out until the end of the month and P/O Sprague was almost shot down by ground fire on the 24th. Fortunately, he managed to return to base uninjured, but the aircraft had been badly hit. Activity

PERSONAL COMBAT REPORT OF P/O LYNCH.

666

DATE:	19th. July. 1942.
SQUADRON.	71 Eagle Sqdn.
TYPE & MARK OF OUR A/C	Spitfire VB.
PLACE OF ATTACK	Between Dunkirk & Nieuport.
TIME ATTACK WAS DELIVERED	About 13.40 hrs.
WEATHER	10/10, cloud base 800'.
OUR CASUALTIES A/C	NIL
" " PERSONNEL.	NIL
E/ CASUALTIES IN AIR COMBAT.	1 FW 190 Destroyed.
GROUND OR SEA TARGET	Nil.

GENERAL REPORT - On 19th July I left Debden 14.40 and joined North Weald Wing (222 Sqdn. in particular) at 15.03 off Dunkirk flying east towards Nieuport. P/O Helgason my No.2 was flying in wide echelon to the left. After flying for some minutes the wing turned to starboard through 180 degs. and flew back along the coast. On the turn my section was between 222 sqdn. and the coast. While flying west along the coast two FW 190's broke cloud in a dive, shallowing the dive out so they approached head on. When within range I fired a short burst at the FW 190 farthest from the coast. He was already firing at someone. As he passed by I looked back and saw him half-roll onto his back. Before turning I looked ahead and saw 4 more FW 190's just below cloud approaching head-on. I pulled up firing a burst into the group which split up as they passed overhead. I then had to pullup into cloud to avoid a section of Spits. When I broke cloud there were no other aircraft in the vicinity and I started to look for my No.2 who has reported engine trouble. Not being able to locate him I returned to base landing at Debden at 16.00 hrs. In view of the possibility of my having fired at the same aircraft that P/O Helgason fired at I only claim one half destroyed. When last seen, on his back, the FW 190 was below 500 feet.

Cine camera was not switched on as I had started out for local flying.

Signature.
P/O Lynch.

Combat report - P/O J.J. lynch of 19 July 1942.

returned to normal in August with 230 sorties flown. On the first day of August, 71 was called to carry out Air Sea Rescue patrols with the sections relieving each other. These were to prove fruitful as enemy aircraft were encountered. Pilot Officer Gray, from California, fired at a Fw190 which disintegrated in mid-air while P/O Sprague gave chase to a Fw190 and fired a short burst. At that moment he was attacked from the rear and had to break away without having time to finish the job. Nevertheless, he was able to see that black smoke had started to come from the Fw190 and it was claimed as damaged. Later that day, Sprague (Red One) crashed on take off after the undercarriage collapsed. He survived unscathed and the Spitfire was found to be repairable. Pilot Officer H.D. Hively (Red Two) from West Virginia continued the sortie alone. The next few days were spent mainly in training, but, sadly, P/O J.F. Helgason was killed while practicing low level attacks on a gun position on the 6th. Until the 19th, the squadron was on the offensive only twice with a *Circus* and a *Roadstead*. Between the 14th and the 20th the unit operated from Gravesend, the base it would occupy for Operation *Jubilee*. The squadron participated in this combined operation with its first sortie taking off at 04.50 to cover the anchorage. Pilot Officer Strickland became separated from the others. He continued on alone and spotted a Fw190 having a sniff around. He attacked it and, before losing it in the gloom, knocked some pieces off it ten miles west of Dieppe before returning to land at Gravesend at 06.00. The rest of the formation was also involved in dogfights and Hawaiian P/O B. Morgan was separated from the others and encountered a Fw190 which made a firing pass at him. He managed to lose it and rejoined the squadron soon after. The CO then ordered him home as his aircraft had a glycol leak. He eventually made a wheels-up landing at Friston. A second sortie was flown soon after, the squadron being airborne at 10.45, Peterson leading again. During this sortie, he damaged a Ju88. The squadron was back on the ground at 12.25 and airborne again at 13.15. Peterson led again and opened fire on a Ju88. Duke-Woolley, at the head of the Debden Wing, saw it go into the sea to confirm Peterson's claim. However, the German rear gunner managed to fire a precise burst into Peterson's Spitfire. Smoke rapidly started to fill the cockpit and he was forced to bale out. Fortunately, he was rescued later in the day. Meanwhile, the other pilots were now involved in fierce combat with the Fw190s. Flight Lieutenant Coen and Pilot Officer M.G.H. McPharlin shared in the probable destruction of a Fw190 that was initially claimed as damaged. However McPharlin was hit in turn and also had to bale out. He was picked by a naval vessel. Finally, the squadron flew a fourth op between 17.15 and 18.55, but this proved uneventful. It participated in a *Circus* with the Wing the following day (*Circus* 206) and then another Wing-strength op the next day. Activity backed off after that until the 27th when the squadron flew a *Circus* to Saint-Omer. Enemy aircraft were encountered and W/C Duke-Woolley and 71 Squadron's new OC, S/L Daymond, each claimed a Fw190, while P/O A.J. Seaman (South Carolina) claimed a probable that was later downgraded to damaged. These were to be the last claims made by 71 Squadron. Sadly, they were balanced against the loss of Sergeant J.E. Evans from Ohio who was shot down and killed by the Fw190s. The squadron flew *Circus* 211 on the 28th, but no claims were made despite numerous combats. On the last day of August, two Spitfires took off at 17.10, P/O Stanley Anderson leading P/O W.D. Taylor from Massachusetts, for a *Rhubarb*. Taylor's aircraft was hit by ground fire while strafing a German flak ship off the Belgian coast and he abandoned his aircraft twenty miles off Blankenberge. He was later observed climbing into his dinghy. The next day, ASR work was carried out and a Defiant from an ASR squadron located him in the morning. However, the weather was closing in and it became impossible for the Walrus to try to pick him up. Another try was made in the afternoon, but Taylor could not be located. He was never seen again. He was to become the last of 71 Squadron's pilots to be killed in action. The next major action for the unit took place on the 5th when it participated with the Wing in a diversion raid for 36 Eighth Air Force B-17 Flying Fortresses, the bombers breaking away to Rouen while the Wing went to Le Tréport. A few enemy aircraft were seen, but did not attack. Two more diversion operations were carried out over the next two days and both were uneventful. The squadron was then placed on readiness for the next few days prior to its pending transfer to the USAAF on the 29th. It was on the 23rd that operational activity resumed with a fruitless scramble in the early hours flown by F/O W.J. Hollander, a Hawaiian, and P/O H.D. Hively. During the next days, the squadron flew some patrols and shipping reconnaissance sorties and avoided any losses before the transfer took place. The last sorties as 71 Squadron were flown on the 27th and involved a shipping reconnaissance led by F/L R.S. Sprague. Two days later, the squadron became the 334th Fighter Squadron of the USAAF.

September 1942, when many of the pilots serving with the squadron were transferring to the USAAF and thus wearing their new American uniforms. Left, Gordon H. Whitlow from Wyoming and, right, Robert L. Priser from Ohio. Both officially transferred on 15.09.42. Whitlow was killed in action nine months later (21.05.43) as a 334th FS member flying a P-47C-5.

Date	Pilot	SN	Origin	Type	Serial	Code	Nb	Cat.
04.09.41	P/O Thomas C. **WALLACE**	RAF No. 61933	(US)/RAF	Bf109	**AB783**		1.0	C
	P/O Gregory A. **DAYMOND**	RAF No. 84657	(US)/RAF	Bf109	**AB811**		1.0	C
	P/O Robert L. **MANNIX**	RAF No. 64864	(US)/RAF	Bf109	**AD123**		1.0	P
07.09.41	F/L Chesley G. **PETERSON**	RAF No. 83706	(US)/RAF	Bf109	**W3627**		1.0	C
18.09.41	F/L Chesley G. **PETERSON**	RAF No. 83706	(US)/RAF	Bf109	**W3627**		1.0	C
19.09.41	P/O Gregory A. **DAYMOND**	RAF No. 84657	(US)/RAF	Bf109	**AB812**		1.0	C
	P/O John **FLYNN**	RAF No. 61956	(US)/RAF	Bf109	**AB907**		1.0	C
21.09.41	P/O Caroll W. **McCOLPIN**	RAF No. 61926	(US)/RAF	Bf109	**AB908**	XR-Y	1.0	C
	P/O Charles W. **TRIBKEN**	RAF No.64866	(US)/RAF	Bf109	**AD123**		1.0	P
27.09.41	F/L Chesley G. **PETERSON**	RAF No. 83706	(US)/RAF	Bf109	**AB810**	XR-V	1.0	P
	P/O Sam A. **MAURIELLO**	RAF No. 87010	(US)/RAF	Bf109	**AB783**		1.0	C
	P/O James J. **CROWLEY** (J.G. DuFour)	RAF No. 89765	(US)/RAF	Bf109	**AD123**		1.0	P
	P/O Ross O. **SCARBOROUGH**	RAF No. 65976	(US)/RAF	Bf109	**AB896**		1.0	C
02.10.41	S/L Stanley T. **MEARES**	RAF No. 37683	RAF	Bf109	**W3819**		1.0	C
	P/O Newton **ANDERSON**	RAF No. 87008	(US)/RAF	Bf109	**AB896**		0.5	C
	P/O Ross O. **SCARBOROUGH**	RAF No. 65976	(US)/RAF		**W3627**		0.5	C
	P/O Arthur F. **ROSCOE**	RAF No. 100530	(US)/RAF	Bf109	**W3708**		1.0	C
	P/O Caroll W. **McCOLPIN**	RAF No. 61926	(US)/RAF	Bf109	**AB908**	XR-Y	2.0	C
16.10.41	P/O Caroll W. **McCOLPIN**	RAF No. 61926	(US)/RAF	Hs126	**AB827**		1.0	C
25.10.41	P/O Ross O. **SCARBOROUGH**	RAF No. 65976	(US)/RAF	Bf109	**AA857**		1.0	C
27.10.41	P/O Caroll W. **McCOLPIN**	RAF No .61926	(US)/RAF	Bf109	**AA857**		2.0	C
07.11.41	P/O Thomas C. **WALLACE**	RAF No. 61933	(US)/RAF	Bf109	**W3708**		1.0	C
09.01.42	P/O Robert S. **SPRAGUE**	RAF No. 103412	(US)/RAF	Fw190	**BL376**		1.0	C
	P/O Eugene M. **POTTER**	RAF No. 100529	(US)/RAF	Fw190	**BL292**		1.0	C
17.04.42	P/O John J. **LYNCH**	RAF No. 103470	(US)/RAF	Ju88	**W3740**		0.5	C
	P/O Leo S. **NOMIS**	RAF No. 107775	(US)/RAF		**BL287**	XR-C	0.5	C
27.04.42	S/L Chesley G. **PETERSON**	RAF No. 83706	(US)/RAF	Fw190	**BL449**		2.0	C
	F/O Oscar H. **COEN**	RAF No. 62244	(US)/RAF	Fw190	**AD564**		0.5	C
	P/O Michael G.H. **McPHARLIN**	RAF No. 89764	(US)/RAF		**W3709**		0.5	C
	F/O Oscar H. **COEN**	RAF No. 62244	(US)/RAF	Fw190	**AD564**		0.5	C
	P/O Michael G.H. **McPHARLIN**	RAF No. 89764	(US)/RAF		**W3709**		0.5	C
	F/O Oscar H. **COEN**	RAF No. 62244	(US)/RAF	Fw190	**AD564**		0.5	C
	P/O Michael G.H. **McPHARLIN**	RAF No. 89764	(US)/RAF		**W3709**		0.5	C
	P/O Arthur F. **ROSCOE**	RAF No. 100530	(US)/RAF	Fw190	**BM293**	XR-W	1.0	P
09.05.42	P/O Arthur F. **ROSCOE**	RAF No. 100530	(US)/RAF	E/A	**AB941**		1.0	P
01.06.42	S/L Chesley G. **PETERSON**	RAF No. 83706	(US)/RAF	Fw190	**BL449**		1.0	C
	F/L Gregory A. **DAYMOND**	RAF No. 84657	(US)/RAF	Fw190	**BL583**		1.0	C
19.07.42	P/O John J. **LYNCH**	RAF No. 103470	(US)/RAF	Fw190			0.5	C
	P/O Joseph F. **HELGASON**	RAF No. 114001	(US)/RAF				0.5	C
01.08.42	P/O James A. **GRAY**	RAF No. 108634	(US)/RAF	Fw190	**AD288**		1.0	C
19.08.42	F/L Oscar H. **COEN**	RAF No. 62244	(US)/RAF	Ju88	**BM293**	XR-W	0.5	P
	P/O Michael G.H. **McPHARLIN**	RAF No. 89764	(US)/RAF		**W3767**		0.5	P
27.08.42	S/L Gregory A. **DAYMOND**	RAF No. 84657	(US)/RAF	Ju88	**BM510**	XR-A	1.0	C

Total: 39.0

Two other American pilots who held a flight commander position with 71 Sqn. Left, Bob Sprague and, right, Sam Mauriello. Sprague transferred in September 1942 and remained with the newly formed 4th FG with the rank of captain and flight leader. Sadly, he was killed in a mid-air collision on 26 November. Sam Mauriello transferred too, but left the 4th FG in December at the end of his tour. He eventually finished the war in the China-Burma-India Theatre. He left the Army after the war.

Summary of the aircraft lost on Operations - 71 Squadron

Date	Pilot	S/N	Origin	Serial	Code	Fate
07.09.41	P/O Hilliard S. FENLOW	RAF No. 61924	(US)/RAF	**AB900**		†
	P/O William H. NICHOLS	RAF No. 86619	(US)/RAF	**AB909**		**PoW**
	F/O Eugene Q. TOBIN	RAF No. 81622	(US)/RAF	**W3801**		†
	P/O Forrest P. DOWLING	RAF No. 100515	(US)/RAF	**AB815**		-
17.09.41	P/O Thomas P. McGERTY	RAF No. 61927	(US)/RAF	**W3509**		†
	P/O William D. GEIGER	RAF No .64862	(US)/RAF	**W3763**	XR-L	**PoW**
13.10.41	P/O Gilmore C. DANIEL	CAN./ J.15016	(US)/RCAF	**AD112**		**PoW**
20.10.41	P/O Oscar H. COEN	RAF No. 62244	(US)/RAF	**AB827**		Eva.
27.10.41	P/O Morris W. FESSLER	RAF No. 88385	(US)/RAF	**AA855**	XR-C	**PoW**
12.04.42	P/O Ben F. MAYS	RAF No. 106509	(US)/RAF	**AB810**	XR-V	†
17.04.42	P/O John J. LYNCH	RAF No. 103470	(US)/RAF	**W3708**		-
25.04.42	P/O Richard McMINN	RAF No. 108641	(US)/RAF	**W3171**		-
27.04.42	P/O James A. GRAY	RAF No. 108634	(US)/RAF	**W3650**		-
	P/O John V. FLYNN	RAF No. 61956	(US)/RAF	**BM206**		†
29.04.42	P/O Leo S. NOMIS	RAF No. 107775	(US)/RAF	**BL287**	XR-C	-
01.06.42	P/O George TEICHEIRA	RAF No. 114074	(US)/RAF	**BM386**		†
02.06.42	P/O Frank G. ZAVAKOS	RAF No. 108645	(US)/RAF	**BM249**	XR-R	†
19.08.42	S/L Chesley G. PETERSON	RAF No. 83706	(US)/RAF	**BM361**	XR-C	-
	P/O Michael G.H. McPHARLIN	RAF No. 89764	(US)/RAF	**W3761**		†
27.08.42	Sgt Jack E. EVANS	CAN./ R.98138	(US)/RCAF	**AD196**	XR-Q	†
31.08.42	P/O William D. TAYLOR	RAF No. 115122	(US)/RAF	**BM305**		†

Total: 21

Frank Zavakos, from Idaho, was the son of Greek immigrants. He had enlisted in the USAAC in October 1940, but, after May 1941, he unexpectedly dropped out to apply to join the RAF through the Clayton Knight Committee. The fact that Greece had just collapsed and been occupied at that time is an indicator as to how he reached his decision while the US was still neutral in the European conflict. Having about 270 hours flying logged helped him speed up his training and he joined 71 Sqn in December 1941 and would serve with the unit until his death on 2 June 1942. *(www.greeks-in-foreign-cockpits.com)*

Summary of the aircraft lost by accident - 71 Squadron

Date	Pilot	S/N	Origin	Serial	Code	Fate
15.10.41	P/O Roger H. **ATKINSON**	RAF No. 102048	(US)/RAF	**AD123**		†
22.10.41	P/O Lawrence A. **CHATTERTON**	RAF No. 100987	(US)/RAF	**AA759**		†
15.11.41	S/L Stanley T. **MEARES**	RAF No. 37683	RAF	**W3963**		†
	P/O Ross O. **SCARBOROUGH**	RAF No. 65976	(US)/RAF	**W3627**		†
09.01.42	P/O William B. **INABINET**	RAF No. 108637	(US)/RAF	**AB783**		†
06.08.42	P/O Joseph F. **HELGASON**	RAF No. 114001	(US)/RAF	**W3709**		†

Total: 6

Victories - confirmed or probable claims: 24.0

First operational sortie:
16.11.41

Last operational sortie:
27.09.42

Number of sorties: 2,749

Total aircraft written-off: 23

Aircraft lost on operations: 21
Aircraft lost in accidents: 2

Squadron code letters:
AV

COMMANDING OFFICERS

S/L Robin P.R. POWELL	RAF No. 33278	RAF	...	17.01.42
S/L Hugh C. KENNARD	RAF No. 40396	RAF	17.01.42	31.07.42
S/L William D. WILLIAMS	RAF No. 78985	RAF	02.08.42	...

SQUADRON USAGE

This unit was formed in May 1941 as the second Eagle Squadron. It made its operational debut in August 1941 and was also initially equipped with Hurricanes. It converted to the Spitfire in October, receiving some Mk.IIs at first, but, in November, the first Mk.V arrived. At that time, the squadron was based at Kirton-in-Lindsey and its British CO, S/L R.P. Powell, had been in command since the unit's formation. He had been awarded the DFC for his service with No. 111 Squadron in May-June 1940. The two flight commanders,

Flight Lieutenants H.C. Kennard and R.C. Wilkinson, were also British and another two experienced pilots who had fought over France or Britain during the previous year. The first Spitfire Mk.Vs, AA903 and AA922, were flight tested on 6 November. More were taken on charge over the following days and subsequently tested. The first operational flights, four aircraft led by Wilkinson on a convoy patrol, were flown on the 16th. Another convoy patrol took off at noon and both were uneventful. The unit's Spitfire Mk.IIs made their last operational sorties the following day. The rest of the month consisted of convoy patrols and useless scrambles, but it is worth noting that the first Mk.V Rhubarb flown by the squadron was a sweep over Holland on the 25th carried out by Virginian P/O R.F. Patterson and New Yorker Sgt J.J. Mooney. Both pilots returned safety, but Mooney's aircraft was slightly damaged.

December 1941 was far from a busy month with just 65 sorties carried out. Bad weather was partially responsible for this result. On the 7th, Pilot Officers Patterson and V.E. Watkins, the latter from California, went on a Rhubarb to the Belgian coast. The target was Knocke, but the two pilots hit the coast twenty miles west at a place called Blankenberge. They became separated for a moment and Watkins ended up returning home alone. Patterson never returned and was

Peter Powell became the first OC of 121 Sqn. A regular RAF officer, he started the war as a flight commander with 111 Sqn flying Hurricanes. He made his first claim as early as January 1940 and more followed over Dunkirk and during the Battle of Britain until he was rested in early August. He received the DFC in May 1940. Promoted to Wing Commander in January 1942, he became the wing leader of the Hornchurch Wing until June when wounds sustained in action kept him away from flying for a while. He later served in Tunisia and was commanding 121 Typhoon Wing at the end of the war.

Succeeding Robin Powell at the head of 121 Sqn, Hugh Kennard was also a veteran of the Battle of Britain, but a Spitfire pilot with 66 Sqn. He had assumed a flight commander position upon the formation of 121 Sqn. Wounded in action on 31 July, he was obliged to relinquish command. No further operational flying positions followed until he took command of 74 Sqn in May 1945 as it was about to convert to the Meteor F.3. *(www.greeks-in-foreign-cockpits.com)*

posted missing. It was later confirmed that he had been killed. The bad luck hung around the squadron as another pilot, Californian P/O K. LeR. Holder, was posted missing from a convoy patrol five days later. Although his body was later recovered, the cause of the crash was never determined.

The new year did not start well for the pilots of 121 when another of their number, P/O J.D. Gilliland from Illinois, was lost in a flying accident on the 8th when operating from Southend. The squadron was now based at Southend after a short stay at North Weald at the end of the 1941. He had taken off at 09.00 with eleven others, F/L Kennard leading, to proceed to Martlesham Heath for a convoy patrol. Sometime after take off, the weather was bad enough to force the formation to return home. Gilliland got lost and crashed in a street in Ipswich. He is believed to have mistaken the fog for cloud. Kennard took over the squadron on the 17th, relinquishing command of his flight to P/O V.E. Watkins. January was otherwise a fairly uneventful month with the squadron being occupied with convoy patrols and only six sorties, of 135 flown that month, being attributed to a single sweep on the 6th. The beginning of February continued in the same vein, but, on the 12th, the squadron participated in the failed attempt to sink two German battlecruisers, *Scharnhorst* and *Gneisenau*, and the heavy cruiser *Prinz Eugen*, as they audaciously ran the gauntlet of the narrow English Channel on their way to German ports during the infamous 'Channel Dash'. The squadron provided air cover for attacking aircraft, but all Spitfires returned to base without having engaged in combat. In the second part of February, 121 continued to carry out convoy patrols, but was engaged more frequently flying *Rhubarbs*, although the Luftwaffe was not seen. With the weather improving, especially after the first week of March, the squadron was airborne more often and 200 sorties were flown that month. On 12 March, the unit took part in a major sweep with the Wing. Heavy flak was experienced between Cassel and Poperinge and probably hit the Spitfire flown by P/O W.L.C. Jones (RCAF), an American from Maryland. He was last seen under control with glycol pouring from his aircraft. He was later reported as a PoW. The next day, the squadron was asked to escort minesweepers. While the patrol itself was uneventful, P/O R.W. Evans stalled and crashed on landing. The aircraft was a write-off and Evans suffered a fractured arm and broken jaw which kept him away from the squadron until mid-June. The same day, major changes occurred in the flight commanders' positions with P/O T.W. Allen, from South Carolina, and P/O C.L. Martin, from Pennsylvania, each receiving their flight lieutenant stripes and assuming the lead of A and B Flights respectively. Until the 23rd, the squadron was involved in uneventful convoy patrols. On the afternoon of the 23rd, a Wing sweep took place, but this time the Luftwaffe was keen to engage the RAF fighters. The other units involved were Nos. 22 and 403 Squadrons. It did not work out well for the attackers with a Fw190, claimed destroyed by P/O Mooney (RCAF), shot down a mile out to sea from Calais. This was the squadron's first confirmed kill since conversion to the Spitfire V. Mooney had also fired earlier at three other Fw190s without result. Pilot Officer W.J. Daley from Texas also fired at three enemy aircraft, but no results were obtained either. Flight Lieutenant Allen had a similar experience with a single Fw190. The next day, the same squadrons (121, 222, 403) were airborne in the early afternoon to accompany eight Bostons to their target at Comines. The Hornchurch, Northholt and Kenley Wings were also part of the game. The Eagles were ordered to protect the Hornchurch Wing and were flying between 15,000 and 16,000 feet when the

Germans appeared. In the ensuing engagement, P/O R.F. Tilley (RCAF) from Florida got into a good position to fire at a Fw190. It was seen belching thick black smoke before diving into a cloud upside down. Tilley claimed it as a probable. Later on, while coming home, Tilley also fired at two other Fw190s, between the target and the French coast, without result. Pilot Officer Daley also used his guns on a Fw190, but was unable to register any hits. In this engagement, 121 did not sustain any direct loss to the Luftwaffe, but P/O L.A. Skinner, from Missouri, made a crash-landing at Deal after running out of fuel. The aircraft did not survive the crash, but Skinner was safe. Before the end of the month, the squadron took part in other Wing sweeps on the 25th, without incident, and on the 27th, but this ended prematurely after a misunderstanding with Control.

On 1 April, the squadron accompanied Nos. 22 and 403 Squadrons to escort twelve Bostons to bomb the docks at Boulogne. The squadron served as high cover, flying at 22,000 feet, but the Luftwaffe did not show up. The unit participated in further sweeps on the 2nd, 3rd, 4th, 8th and 10th, but those proved rather uneventful. Another sweep was flown on the 12th with the Debden and Hornchurch Wings also taking part. The task was, once again, an escort for twelve Bostons, but, contrary to the previous raids, at least as far as 121 Squadron was concerned, the enemy was engaged. The North Weald Wing was acting as close escort to the Bostons and 121 was flying at 10,000 feet when Fw190s intercepted the formation around Hazebrouck. Fierce combat ensued and in about ten minutes the Eagles had made six claims. Flight Lieutenant T.W. Allen, from South Carolina, claimed one probable and one damaged, while P/O L.A. Skinner from Missouri damaged two. The CO and Californian P/O J.B. Mahon claimed one damaged Fw190 each. These successes were claimed for no loss even though the aircraft of P/O Edner (Minnesota) returned with some flak damage. One of Skinner's claims was confirmed as destroyed two days later. Another sweep was carried out the next day, but the Germans were not sighted. Yet another was flown on the 14th and P/O Mooney was able to fire two bursts at a Bf109, but did not have the chance to see how effective he had been. On the 15th, the squadron was able to file some claims. After one diversionary sweep in the morning, 121 took part in another Wing sweep to escort Hurricane fighter-bombers. Combat occurred around Calais and Saint-Omer and two Fw190s were claimed destroyed, one by P/O S.R. Edner and one by P/O Skinner. Edner dived from 20,000 feet to 9,000 feet to attack his future victim, closing in to 400 yards before firing. He missed with his first three second burst so continued to follow the 190 to 7,000 feet where he fired for another three seconds and caused the Fw190 to burst into flames before it crashed into the ground. Skinner flew a similar attack and saw his Fw190 crash into the sea after a three second burst from 75 yards astern. Flight Lieutenant Allen got himself in to a good position to fire at another Fw190, but he did not see the results and only made a claim for a damaged Fw190 after his gun camera film was examined. The next day, the squadron was airborne again for one another sweep, but this time things went wrong as P/O R.V. Brossmer, from New York State, crashed on take off. His Spitfire turned over, but he was dragged out with nothing worse than cuts and bruises. The aircraft was repaired. Soon after, S/L Kennard had to return home when his canopy came off. He was followed by F/L Martin and

Pilots of 121 Sqn marching for the camera with the 'Stars and Stripes' flag in the background. This photo was taken for propaganda purposes at the end of November just a few days before the USA entered war.
The pilots who can be identified are, from left to right: M.L. Stepp from California (killed 30.09.43 with the USAAF), L.A. Skinner from Missouri (PoW 28.04.42), D.W. McLeod from Massachusetts, behind, K.L. Holder from California (killed 12.12.41), H.C. Kennard, A Flight OC - British, F.A. Gamble from Tennessee (killed 03.05.42), S/L R.P.P. Powell, OC - British, V.A. Parker from Texas, R.E. McHan from Nebraska (who would not transfer to the USAAF), J.J. Lynch from Ohio, C.L. Martin from Pennsylvania, W.L.C. Jones from Maryland (PoW 08.03.42), R.F. Patterson from Virginia (killed 07.12.41) and W.J. Daley from Texas with head down (killed 10.09.44 with the USAAF).

Two pilots conversing after returning from an op: John Mooney from New York (left) and Don McLeod from Massachusetts. Mooney, a key pilot, was earmarked for greater responsibility and would likely have become CO if he had not been killed in action as a flight commander on 16 June 1942. McLeod, like Reade Tilley, left the squadron in March 1942 for Malta where he was severely wounded in combat. He returned to the UK at the end of July 1942 and transferred to the USAAF in September, but did not serve with the 4th FG.

No.121 Squadron soldiered on with Spitfire Mk.Vs for the last ten months of its brief existence. This is a very well known photo of BM590/AV-R, 'Olga', in flight. It was regularly flown by Gilbert O. Halsey, from Oklahoma, who joined the squadron in February 1942. At age 32, Halsey was the oldest Eagle pilot when he transferred to the USAAF in September 1942. He remained with the 335th FS until the end of his tour.

P/O J.I. Brown (Illinois) who both returned early with engine trouble. On the 17th, the squadron was tasked with two ops. The first was an uneventful diversionary Wing sweep just before midday. They returned to the same area in the middle of the afternoon, flying as top cover at 27,000 feet. This time the Luftwaffe rose to fight. A melee soon developed and when the Germans extricated themselves, they had had the advantage as none of the participating Eagle pilots were able to make claims, but one pilot, F/Sgt F.C. Austin (RCAF) from California, was missing. After this intensive first fortnight, the pressure eased for the next few days and little flying was performed (none over the Continent). Bad weather was to blame and the pilots took the opportunity to rest. Ops resumed on the 24th. The Wing combined its strength with the Debden Wing and took off in the direction of France to escort twelve Bostons to attack the harbour and oil installations at Flushing in Belgium. After successfully escorting the bombers, Pilot Officers Daley and Skinner spotted what they thought to be a Ju52 transport aircraft. They peeled off, attacked it several times, and it began to trail white smoke and shed pieces. From above, the wing leader, W/C Scott-Malden, and P/O Allen watched as the enemy aircraft caught fire and went into the sea. Later on, when they compared notes and checked the photos of their cine-gun film, Daley and Skinner discovered they had shot down a venerable Junkers W-34. It was, however, credited as a Ju52. Another sweep was undertaken the next day and the Luftwaffe tried to intercept the raid. Only P/O Mooney was able to fire at a Fw190, but, as he did not see any result, no claim was made. However, P/O B.C. Downs from Texas encountered engine trouble and was forced to bale out over the sea four miles off Ramsgate. He was not picked up, but was able to paddle his dinghy safely to shore and was soon back with the squadron. Another dogfight occurred on the 28th during which F/O S.R. Edner made a claim against a Fw190. It was initially claimed as a probable, but was later downgraded to damaged. The Germans once again achieved a clear advantage over the Americans and P/O C.G. Bodding, from Kansas, was shot down and seen to bale out. Sadly, he was too low and was killed. It was not the only loss as P/O Skinner also had to bale out. He ended up in captivity. Another sweep was carried out on the 29th and was followed by three more on the 30th, one in the morning and two in the afternoon, but nothing came of those raids. In all, 426 sorties were flown in April and the squadron also celebrated flying 1000 sorties since its formation.

May was also intense even though the number of sorties decreased, 386 in May against April's 426. The squadron flew over French or Belgian territory almost every day of the month. The Luftwaffe was not seen each time and, when combat did occur, claims were not always forthcoming. On 4 May, near Le Havre, S/L Kennard shot at two Bf109s without result, as did F/L Allen against a Bf109. Pilot Officer Daley fired at another Bf109 and observed no result even though Allen and P/O Mahon saw the German spinning down pouring white smoke. The combat was fierce, however, but the Germans got the advantage over the Spitfires and two pilots were posted missing – Pilot Officers R.W. Freiberg from Minnesota and R.V. Brossmer from New York City. Flight Lieutenant Martin saw Freiberg's aircraft diving towards the sea about fifteen miles off Le Havre. He tried to call him over the radio, but got no answer. As for Brossmer, he was last seen by P/O Mooney leaving the French coast.

Until the 11th, the squadron was sent over the Continent every day, but no combats eventuated. The squadron was released from 13.00 on the 11th and, during the next few days, bad weather prevented further activity. The Eagles were airborne again on the 14th then released the next day because of the weather. Operations resumed on the 16th, but the day's Rhubarb was uneventful. The following day the squadron took off twice for sweeps to Boulogne with Nos. 222 and 331 Squadrons. For the first sweep, the Wing returned without incident, but, on the second one, while near Saint-Omer, P/O Edner saw a Fw190 and attacked from 190 yards with a one second burst. The Fw190 exploded. Almost immediately after, it was the turn of P/O Daley to spot and engage a Fw190. The attack was made from behind and above and P/O Daley fired a three second burst. The enemy fighter caught fire and was not seen again. Both claims were accepted as destroyed, while Pilot Officers Mooney and Mahon each claimed a Fw190 as damaged. On 20 May six aircraft were sent on a shipping reconnaissance with the aim of flying around Brankenburg. Finding nothing, they decided to fly towards Walcheren and soon after saw a German patrol vessel which opened fire at them. The six Spitfires dove from 6,000 feet to make several firing passes. The patrol boat was left severely damaged and disappeared before escorting Bf109s, which were flying too far away, could come to the rescue. Operations continued over the following days and another boat was attacked on the 26th. The next day, two minesweepers escorted by a destroyer became the target of the Eagles. They were attacked and damaged, but Bf109s made an appearance and went after P/O Daley and Sgt Vance. Daley attacked one of them and soon one Bf109 was seen to crash into the sea. Vance claimed another as damaged. Vance was not the only one to claim a Bf109 damaged as P/O Mahon did the same. The squadron flew operationally on the 28th and the 30th, but nothing of interest was reported. On the 31st, the North Weald Wing proceeded on a shipping reconnaissance off the coast of Flushing and two minesweepers were eventually attacked and damaged. In doing so, F/L Allen, who had made a steep dive attack, struck the water and ricocheted up to about 1000 feet. He announced over the R/T that his aircraft was coming apart and that he proposed to ditch at 100 mph. He did so at a rather steep angle and was not seen to emerge from the Spitfire, which sank immediately. It is thought that he may have been hit in the engine during the second attack as P/O 'Barry' Mahon stated that he saw glycol streaming from Allen's aircraft.

On 1 June, 121 took part in a Rodeo in the morning and a *Circus* in the afternoon. Operations continued over the next few days with 111 sorties carried out up to the 5th. No operations were flown during the next two days due to bad weather, but the squadron returned over the French coast on the 8th for a *Rodeo*. Near Saint-Omer, the unit engaged some Fw190s and F/L Mooney, the new B Flight CO, was the first to make a claim when he sent a Fw190 crashing to the ground. Immediately after this one, he attacked another Fw190 and shot it down in flames in a couple of seconds. At the same time, P/O Mahon sealed the fate of two other Fw190s, both being claimed as destroyed. These victories were the first double claims made by squadron pilots since the unit's formation. Also pleasing was that all Spitfires returned to base. On 14 June, the squadron flew a shipping reconnaissance and was just outside Ostend when they saw an armed trawler sailing four miles from the coast off Walcheren. Squadron Leader Kennard made two attacks at deck height as the vessel opened fire with machine guns mounted on the stern. Kennard then ordered the squadron to join in. The squadron made two more passes and eventually silenced the guns. During the second attack, a violent explosion was seen on the stern and thick black smoke issued from the vessel. It was seen to list heavily to starboard, decrease its speed and make for shore. After a convoy patrol on the morning of the 16th, F/L Mooney and P/O 'Sed' Edner headed out on a Rhubarb. They took off at 12.20 and travelled towards Ostend where a freight train was observed. They attacked it from astern, F/O Edner firing a four second burst. This resulted in the train being brought

Jackson B. Mahon, who hailed from California, arrived at the squadron in December 1941. He became one of the most successful pilots of the unit by claiming a brace of victories, two double kills, in ten days. On 19 August 1942, during the Dieppe raid, he shot down his fifth opponent, but was shot down himself and thus prevented from lodging the claim. He was, however, picked up by the Germans and made a prisoner, during which time he was awarded the DFC. After the war he returned to California where he became the personal pilot, and eventually the manager, of Errol Flynn and spent the rest of his career in the movie business.

to a standstill and it appeared as though the driver had been killed. Immediately after this attack, F/L Mooney disappeared so Edner called him on his R/T, but it had gone u/s. He then circled the train twice, to see if there was any sign of F/L Mooney, but to no avail. Mooney was replaced at the head of B Flight by W.J. Daley. The squadron lost a second Spitfire in June, but by accident, when, on the 23rd, Virginian P/O J.M. Osborne hit the Blackwater River off Osea Island, Essex, while involved in low flying practice with five other aircraft. He survived and was picked up by fishing boats soon after. More operations were flown over the Continent until the end of the month, but nothing of note was reported. June ended quite smoothly with some uneventful convoy patrols. July, however, would be the busiest month for the squadron with 528 sorties carried out. Nevertheless, the first week was quiet and no major operations were flown. On the 8th, P/O G.O. Halsey (Oklahoma) and Sgt A.C. Stanhope (of French parentage) were scrambled at 07.10 and vectored to intercept a lone Ju88. They spotted it off Dunkirk and gave chase. It was not until the Junkers was over Cap Gris Nez that both pilots were able to attack. Halsey fired a four second burst from 400 yards line astern, but observed no results. Stanhope then fired from the same distance. At first it seemed impossible to catch the Junkers, but Stanhope gave it another burst from astern which caused it to weave. This gave him the opportunity to close in. Stanhope saw the rear gunner firing at him so fired another short burst from 300 yards to silence him. Closing in, he fired again from 80-90 yards and observed orange flashes coming from the port engine and thick smoke trailing from it. The Junkers then went into a cloud and Stanhope waited for it to emerge. He fired a final burst when it did and expended his ammunition. The two American pilots returned to base where they claimed the Ju88 as damaged.

Offensive operations were resumed from the 12th with a Rodeo followed by Rhubarbs on the 14th and 15th. The *Rhubarb* on the 15th was followed by a *Roadstead*. No enemy aircraft were encountered, but this was not the case for the *Rodeo* of the 19th as F/L S.R. Edner claimed a Fw190 as damaged. Only one other claim for a damaged aircraft was filed on the 30th (F/L W. Daley) despite numerous ops flown over the previous ten days. During that period, when eighty sorties were flown, the squadron did not suffer any losses, but one Spitfire was damaged by flak on the 22nd and its pilot, F/Sgt J.M. Sanders (RCAF) from Tennessee, was slightly injured in his right hand. On 31 July, twelve pilots took off at 14.10 for a *Circus*. The squadron was led by the CO. Landfall was made at Berck-sur-Mer and rendezvous with the North Weald and Tangmere Wings was made at Pevensey Bay. They had to escort six Bostons to Abbeville. The Luftwaffe decided to intervene and rose to intercept. The Eagles did not wait to be attacked and chased after several Fw190s encountered. The harvest of victories that followed was to be the best ever claimed by the unit to date. The CO claimed one Fw190 destroyed, while F/L Edner and Mahon each scored two destroyed. Two pilots opened their score that day. Sergeant W.P. Kelly from New York State claimed one aircraft destroyed and F.R. Boyles claimed a probable Fw190. These victories were obtained at a cost, however, as P/O N.D. Young, from Oregon, who had been with the squadron for only two weeks, was lost. The CO was also injured and had to crash land at Lynpne where he was taken to the hospital at Maidstone. While he recovered from his injuries, it put an end to his command and he did not lead another operational unit before the end of the war. He was replaced by British S/L W.D. Williams, posted from 122 Squadron, from August 2 onwards. In August, the squadron was airborne operationally for 25 days out of 31 and flew just over 300 operational sorties. Without a doubt the main event of the month was the unit's participation in Operation *Jubilee* on the 19th. Up to that date, the squadron had little to report upon return from their ops. On the famous day over Dieppe, the first operation was carried out in the morning, taking off at 08.40, in company with No. 19 Squadron. They patrolled over Dieppe at 5,000 feet and, less than 45 minutes after taking off, 121 was involved in various dogfights with Fw190s. The squadrons were split up and the pilots returned to base one by one or in pairs. It didn't take long to observe that three pilots were missing – P/O J.L. Taylor from Indiana, and Californians P/O J.B. Mahon and P/O G.B. Fetrow. Soon after, good news came from Fetrow who had been obliged to bale out over England, his aircraft on fire following hits from German fighters. Later on, it was discovered that Mahon had been shot down and become a PoW after he had shot down his fifth enemy aircraft (that he could not file as a claim). Sadly, for Taylor, the news was not good as he was presumed dead following a possible collision with a Fw190. On the other hand, one confirmed victory and two probables, along with a damaged claim by P/O F.D. Smith, a Texan, almost balanced the ledger. Despite its losses, the squadron was airborne again at 11.50, again with 19 Squadron, but the weather deteriorated quickly forcing the pilots to fly below 2,500 feet and, therefore, in range of light flak. One Spitfire, F/L Daley's, was hit. While 19 Squadron engaged the enemy, 121 was not as lucky and came close to losing a fourth Spitfire when Daley's engine stopped a few seconds after being hit. He was preparing to bale out when the engine restarted. A third op was carried out in the late afternoon, but proved uneventful except that P/O J.M. Osborne crashed back at base when the undercarriage collapsed on landing. Following Dieppe, 121 continued to fly operational sorties, almost 95 of them before the end of the month, including 29 on the 24th. However, no further combats or losses were reported.

In September, operational activity decreased pending the future transfer to the USAAF at the end of the month. The number of sorties was almost cut by half. On 1 September, two sections received orders to intercept a lone Ju88. The German reconnaissance bomber was sighted once, but it disappeared into cloud and was not seen again. Early in the month, F/L Edner received notification that he had been awarded the DFC, the last of four pilots, following Kennard, Daley and Mahon, to be so awarded while flying with 121 Squadron. The first sweep of September was performed on the 5th towards Abbeville, but was uneventful. The squadron flew a diversionary sweep the next day and, on the 7th, engaged the Luftwaffe, but no claim was made by the two pilots who nevertheless were able to get in to good positions to open fire (Pilot Officers Fentrow and Stanhope). That was to be the last engagement against the Luftwaffe for the squadron as it flew convoy patrols or shipping recces from then on. During one such sortie on the 21st, 121 lost its last aircraft and pilot when New Jersey native P/O Slater was hit in the glycol tank by fire from a flak ship. He was flying with P/O W.P. Kelly (RCAF) and they had attacked the ship and left it burning. Kelly saw Slater, who was posted missing, crash into the sea. Two days later, the squadron moved to Debden to become the 335th Fighter Squadron of the 4th Fighter Group, USAAF.

Claims - 121 Squadron (Confirmed and Probable)

Date	Pilot	SN	Origin	Type	Serial	Code	Nb	Cat.
23.03.42	P/O John J. **Mooney**	Can./ J.15024	(us)/RCAF	Fw190	AA904	AV-W	1.0	C
24.03.42	P/O Reade F. **Tilley**	Can./ J.15011	(us)/RCAF	Fw190	AD463		1.0	P
12.04.42	P/O LeRoy A. **Skinner**	RAF No. 101460	(us)/RAF	Fw190	AD501		1.0	C
	F/L Thomas W. **Allen**	Can./ J.15015	(us)/RCAF	Fw190	BL986		1.0	P
15.04.42	P/O LeRoy A. **Skinner**	RAF No. 101460	(us)/RAF	Fw190	W3804		1.0	C
	F/O Selden R. **Edner**	RAF No. 64860	(us)/RAF	Fw190	AA903	AV-N	1.0	C
27.04.42	P/O William J. **Daley**	RAF No. 101457	(us)/RAF	Ju52*	P8794	AV-Q	0.5	C
	P/O LeRoy A. **Skinner**	RAF No. 101460	(us)/RAF		W3804		0.5	C
17.05.42	P/O William J. **Daley**	RAF No. 101457	(us)/RAF	Fw190	R6890		1.0	C
	F/O Selden R. **Edner**	RAF No. 64860	(us)/RAF	Fw190	AA903	AV-N	1.0	C
27.05.42	P/O William J. **Daley**	RAF No. 101457	(us)/RAF	Bf109	BL986		1.0	C
08.06.42	F/L John J. **Mooney**	Can./ J.15024	(us)/RCAF	Fw190	AD423		2.0	C
	P/O Jackson B. **Mahon**	RAF No. 108640	(us)/RAF	Fw190	?		2.0	C
31.07.42	Sgt William P. **Kelly**	Can./ R.89902	(us)/RCAF	Bf109	BM581	AV-P	1.0	C
	P/O Frank R. **Boyles**	RAF No. 111571	(us)/RAF	Bf109	AA841		1.0	C
	F/L Selden R. **Edner**	RAF No. 64860	(us)/RAF	Fw190	EN918	AV-X	2.0	C
	P/O Jackson B. **Mahon**	RAF No. 108640	(us)/RAF	Fw190	BM405	AV-J	2.0	C
	S/L Hugh C. **Kennard**	RAF No. 40396	RAF	Bf109	BL234		1.0	C
19.08.42	Sgt Leon McF. **Blanding**	Can./ R.79288	(us)/RCAF	Fw190	EN822		1.0	P
	F/L Selden R. **Edner**	RAF No. 64860	(us)/RAF	Fw190	EN918	AV-X	1.0	C
	P/O Gilbert O. **Halsey**	RAF No. 112619	(us)/RAF	Fw190	BM590	AV-R	1.0	P

Total: 24.0

*Actually a Junkers W34 but credited as a Ju52

Summary of the aircraft lost on Operations - 121 Squadron

Date	Pilot	S/N	Origin	Serial	Code	Fate
07.12.41	P/O Richard F. **Patterson**	Can./ J.2928	(us)/RCAF	**W3711**	AV-H	†
12.12.41	P/O Kenneth LeR. **Holder**	raf No. 118173	(us)/RAF	**AA871**	AV-D	†
08.03.42	P/O William L.C. **Jones**	Can./ J.15052	(us)/RCAF	**AB206**	AV-S	†
09.03.42	P/O Roy W. **Evans**	raf No. 108632	(us)/RAF	**BL465**		-
24.03.42	P/O LeRoy A. **Skinner**	raf No. 101460	(us)/RAF	**BL963**		
12.04.42	P/O Selden R. **Edner**	raf No. 64860	(us)/RAF	**BL447**		
17.04.42	F/Sgt Frederick C. **Austin**	Can./ R.58580	(us)/RCAF	**AD498**	AV-C	†
25.04.42	P/O Bruce C. **Downs**	raf No. 108631	(us)/RAF	**AB793**		-
28.04.42	P/O Carl G. **Bodding**	raf No. 108628	(us)/RAF	**AD289**	AV-J	†
	P/O LeRoy A. **Skinner**	raf No. 101460	(us)/RAF	**W3804**		**PoW**
04.05.42	P/O Ralph W. **Freiberg**	raf No. 110340	(us)/RAF	**P8794**	AV-Q	†
	P/O Robert V. **Brossmer**	raf No. 106352	(us)/RAF	**AD460**	AV-P	†
31.05.42	F/L Thomas W. **Allen**	Can./ J.15015	(us)/RCAF	**W3645**		†
16.06.42	F/L John J. **Mooney**	Can./ J.15024	(us)/RCAF	**W3841**		†
31.07.42	S/L Hugh C. **Kennard**	raf No. 40396	RAF	**BL234**		-
	P/O Norman D. **Young**	raf No. 116163	(us)/RAF	**AA732**		†
19.08.42	P/O James LaR. **Taylor**	raf No. 110338	(us)/RAF	**AD569**		†
	P/O Jackson B. **Mahon**	raf No. 108640	(us)/RAF	**BM405**	AV-J	**PoW**
	P/O Gene B. **Fetrow**	raf No. 113977	(us)/RAF	**BM401**		-
	P/O Julian M. **Osborne**	raf No. 112312	(us)/RAF	**P8589**		-
21.09.42	P/O John T. **Slater***	raf No. 116645	(us)/RAF	**P8339**	AV-I	†

Total: 21

*As per 121 ORB, but Slater is officially a USAAF loss as O-885133, having made his transfer on 16 September.

Summary of the aircraft lost by accident - 121 Squadron

Date	Pilot	S/N	Origin	Serial	Code	Fate
08.01.42	P/O Jack D. **Gilliland**	raf No. 106510	(us)/RAF	**W3240**	AV-X	†
23.06.42	P/O Julian M. **Osborne**	raf No. 112312	(us)/RAF	**BL490**	AV-P	-

Total: 2

No. 121 Squadron in August 1942 shortly before becoming the 335th FS, USAAF:
Pilot Officer J.M. Osborne from Virginia shares his experience of a dogfight, following a fighter sweep, with other members of the Eagle Squadron. Left to right are: F.D. Smith from Texas, J.M. Sanders from Tennessee, D.A. Young from Kansas, P/O Osborne, S/L W.D. Williams (RAF), C.V. Padget from Maryland, G.B. Fetrow from California, F.R. Vance (RCAF) from Washington D.C. who did not transfer (killed 13.07.43), G.O. Halsey from Oklahoma, P/O F.R. Boyles born in Burma from American parentage (with the cigarette and a shoulder badge 'U.S.A.' instead of the usual Eagle badge – killed 28.07.43 with the USAAF), S.R. Edner from Minnesota (just visible), W.J. Daley from Texas, J.R. Happel from New Jersey, and J.B. Mahon from California (PoW 19.08.42).

Victories - confirmed or probable claims: 21.50

Number of sorties: 1,740

First operational sortie:
06.01.42
Last operational sortie:
20.08.43

Total aircraft written-off: 18

Aircraft lost on operations: 12
Aircraft lost in accidents: 6

Squadron code letters:
MD

COMMANDING OFFICERS

S/L Eric H. THOMAS	RAF No. 39138	RAF	...	01.08.42
F/L Do,ald B.M. BLAKESLEE (*TEMP.*)	CAN./ J.4551	(US)/RCAF	01.08.42	01.09.42
S/L Caroll W. McCOLPIN	RAF No. 61926	(US)/RAF	01.09.42	...

SQUADRON USAGE

The final RAF squadron to be formed with American pilots, No. 133 (Eagle) Squadron had had a quiet existence when the first Spitfire Mk.V arrived. Formed at the end of July 1941, the squadron became operational on Hurricane Mk.IIs which were soon replaced with Spitfire IIs. Operating from Eglinton in the autumn of 1941, they actually saw no action. When the unit moved to Kirton-in-Lindsey on 2 January 1942, it was under the command of a British officer, S/L Eric H. Thomas, a Battle of Britain veteran. Of the two flight commanders, only one was American, Charles E. Bateman from Massachusetts, B Flight, while A Flight was commanded by F/L Hugh A.S. Johnstone. At Kirton-in-Lindsey, the squadron was re-equipped with the Spitfire Mk.VA, making it, therefore, one of the very few operational units to be fully equipped with this early version of the Mk.V.

The first sorties, uneventful convoy patrols, were carried out on 6 January. Besides a handful of uneventful scrambles or dusk patrols, convoy patrols were the norm for the squadron in January.

No flying could be performed during the first four days of February due to a continuous snowfall. Operational activity resumed on 5 February and the first combats ever for the squadron took place that day. The first involved a Ju88 sighted by F/L Johnstone at 09.30 while he was up conducting a weather test. The Junkers was flying north up the coast ten miles north of Spurn Head. Johnstone started to chase it, but the Junkers disappeared into cloud and was lost. The day wasn't over yet, however. In the afternoon, the squadron carried out its regular convoy patrols. In the middle of the afternoon, Johnstone and his number two, P/O M.A. Jackson from Texas, and F/L McColpin (who had recently taken over B Flight) teamed with Sgt W.C. Wicker (RCAF) from Illinois, were 45 minutes into their patrol when they spotted three Dornier 217s trying to bomb the convoy. The Dorniers were attacked by the 133 Squadron pilots, but also by other fighters from the escort, in this case, the Hurricanes of No. 253 Squadron. One Dornier was quickly accounted for and seen to crash by the

> Squadron Leader E.H. Thomas was commanding 133 Sqn when the unit received its first Spitfire Mk.Vs. The Battle of Britain veteran had previously led 611 Sqn before being posted to 133 in November 1941. He left 133 Sqn in August 1942 to become wing leader of the Biggin Hill and, later, Hornchurch Wings until November. Because of health problems, he had to relinquish his commission in September 1944, but with a DSO and DFC and Bar to his name.

Top and below, the CO's aircraft MD-A/BM263. Note the wheels painted with the RAF roundel and the unusual positioning of the squadron leader's pennant under the nose.

Don Blakeslee's arrival in the Eagle squadron was kind of accidental. A native of Ohio, he crossed the border in July 1940 to join the RCAF. He then continued his selection and training until he was posted to a Canadian fighter unit, 411 Sqn, based in the UK upon its formation in June 1941. In November he was posted to another Canadian squadron, 401, where he made his first claims. By the summer of 1942, he had gained very valuable experience and was posted to 133 Sqn when it was suffering from a lack of experienced pilots. He took command of B Flight following 'Red' McColpin's departure for the USA to participate in a bond drive for ten weeks. Without that, Blakeslee may have never been connected with the Eagle squadrons. He transferred to the USAAF and would eventually lead the 4th FG in 1944. He continued to serve the USAAF and USAF after the war and participated in the Korean War at the head of a F-84 wing. While he did lead 133 Sqn in action, he was never officially appointed as its OC even though he had proven he had the skills for this position.

escort vessel at the rear of the convoy. The victory was shared by Johnstone and Jackson, but also with two pilots of 253 Squadron. 'Red' McColpin returned to base with his guns empty and a report for a damaged Do217 to fill in. However, in the meantime, the squadron lost one of its Spitfires during a training flight when F/Sgt F.C. Austin (RCAF), an American from California, hit a snowdrift on take off. The Spitfire was too damaged to consider for repair. The rest of the month consisted of patrols and a few scrambles, but nothing really happened for the unit after the 5th. In all, the squadron carried out 306 sorties in February, its best total since formation. This total included some sorties flown by Spitfire VBs (aircraft borrowed from other units at Kirton and not officially allocated).

In March, uneventful convoy patrols basically took up the entire month. However, March was marked by the loss of the first pilot flying a Spitfire V. On the 16th, P/O H.C. Brown, a Canadian-born American, took off at 08.25 with F/Sgt C.W Harp (RCAF) from Alabama for a weather test over the Channel to establish whether convoy patrols could be safely conducted. When at a spot fifteen miles east of Mablethorpe, Harp called up Brown to tell him that he was going to climb as visibility was practically nil. There was no answer and it was assumed that Brown had crashed into the sea at that moment or just before. In March, the number of sorties dropped to less than 200. For the first half of April, the squadron carried out the usual convoy patrols with, on some days, a constant patrol maintained throughout the day. In this period of time, there were no encounters with the enemy. On the rare occasion the squadron was called to scramble, either as a precaution for an incoming raid or to investigate unidentified aircraft, the intercepted aircraft proved to be friendly in each case. While flying these uneventful patrols, training continued. On 3 April, two Spitfires collided during a training flight. While both pilots managed to abandon their aircraft, the parachute of P/O S.F. Whedon, an American from Wisconsin, caught a strong gust of wind and caused him to lose his footing, fall backwards, and fatally strike his head on a rock. On 16 April, the squadron participated in two fighter sweeps, led by W/C Walker, with the two other squadrons of the Wing, Nos. 19 and 412 Squadrons. Both were uneventful. After a further couple of patrols, 133 returned to the offensive with the Wing on the 24th, but, once more, the Luftwaffe could not be found when the Wing swept the north coast of France and into Belgium. The next day, the first Spitfire VB was lost in an accident when the aircraft flown by Sgt G.E. Eichar (RCAF) from Iowa was hit by a wind gust on landing. It bounced, stalled and an undercarriage leg collapsed. The Spitfire was declared damaged beyond economic repair. The following day, the 26th, the squadron took part in two other Wing ops over the same area as previous sweeps. During the first one early in the afternoon, 133 saw enemy aircraft beyond the edge of their formation, but did not engage. Later in the afternoon, the Wing returned over the French coast and, over Boulogne, it was attacked by Fw190s. Flight Lieutenant McColpin managed to shoot down one of them, it was seen crashing into the sea, and, in the melee, the squadrons were split up. On 27 April, the squadron, part of the Wing with Nos. 616 and 412 Squadrons, left West Malling to make a rendezvous at Southend with the North Weald Wing. The Wing was acting as top cover with 133 flying high cover for *Circus* 142. On reaching Ostend, about thirty Fw190s were seen above at 21,000 feet. Blue Section was engaged by some of them when they dived and, in the ensuing melee, P/O R.L. Pewitt, from Texas, claimed one Fw190 as probably destroyed. At the same time White Section was attacked from below and P/O W.H. Baker, another Texan, chased a Fw190 down to 10,000 feet, firing a long burst. Baker also claimed it as probably destroyed. Shortly after this, the Wing turned for home and F/Sgt W.C. Wicker from Illinois was heard over the radio reporting that he had been hit. Posted missing on arrival at base, his body was washed up at Dover two days later. No more offensive operations were carried out before the end of the month, only regular patrols. On 29 April, the CO took off with P/O E. Doorly from New Jersey at 02.30 for a night patrol. They encountered a Do217 and it was engaged, Doorly claiming it as damaged. He was hit by return fire, however, probably in the glycol system as the engine temperature began to rise almost immediately and, before he could reach the coast, the engine stopped, forcing him to abandon the Spitfire six miles south-east of Church Fenton. He landed safely. April saw the squadron's real entry into the air war with the first combat with German fighters over the Continent producing encouraging results. The squadron was now fully equipped with the Mk.VB.

No operational flights were performed during the first days of May as the squadron was involved in its move to Biggin Hill which it completed on the 3rd. The first operation, a fighter sweep with the rest of the Wing (Nos. 72, 124 and 401 Squadrons), was carried out on the 7th. The squadron acted as top cover for six Bostons detailed to bomb Ostend. No enemy was seen and the op was conducted without incident. Two more sweeps were flown on the 9th, another on the 10th, and, again, all aircraft returned with nothing to report even though, on the raid on the 10th, the enemy was seen, but not engaged (the squadron ran into a bunch of Bf109s flying at 21,000 feet, but the chase was abandoned when the Germans put their noses down and dived away). On the 9th, 133 celebrated its one thousandth sortie since formation. It returned to the north coast of France one week later and this time luck was with the Eagles. The Luftwaffe accepted the engagement and, by the time it was over, F/L McColpin was able to fill in two claims for Bf109s (one confirmed and one probable) and P/O M.S. Morris, from Oklahoma, one probable. This was achieved without losses on the Eagles' side. The next day, the squadron was engaged by six German fighters over the Dieppe area. While the CO and Californian P/O G.B. Sperry were able to get into good firing positions, no claims were made. The result was totally different on the following day, the 19th. During another sweep over the Fécamp-Le Tréport area, the Luftwaffe intercepted the Wing and, in the ensuing combat, F/Sgt C.W. Harp, from Alabama, claimed two Fw190s destroyed, while P/O M.S. Morris from Oklahoma added a Bf109 destroyed and another damaged to his tally. Pilot Officer Sperry was also happy to return with a claim to fill in, a damaged Bf109, even though he would have to share it with the Biggin Hill Wing. Two pilots, however, did not make it home. Pilot Officer R.L. Pewitt from Texas was seen to go down with two fighters on his tail about ten miles south of Beachy Head. His aircraft was hit and severely damaged and he crashed into the sea off Beachy Head. He was rescued, but died of head injuries before being admitted to hospital. The other pilot posted missing, and believed to have been shot down, was P/O D.R. Florance, a Canadian-born American, whose body was never recovered. After a period of patrols, 133 returned, uneventfully as it turned out, to the offensive on the 23rd. The next day, Pilot Officers M.E. Jackson from Texas and E.D. Taylor from Oklahoma were patrolling off the Dungeness-Hastings area when they spotted two Bf109s returning to the French coast. They ran after them and Jackson closed in enough to be able to fire a short burst and damage one of the fleeing fighters. Later that day, the squadron was in action for another sweep over the Hardelot-Saint-Omer area, but, while many enemy aircraft was seen, it was unable to engage. Before the end of the month, 133 took part in six more sweeps over France and its tally increased with one Fw190 damaged on the 27th (S/L E.H. Thomas) and another, by P/O Taylor, on the 31st during the last sweep of the month. This latter claim was thin compensation for the loss of two pilots, P/O M.S. Morris and Texan P/O W.K. Ford, who were both shot down and killed by Fw190s. Pilot Officer Doorly's Spitfire was also damaged during the combat, but managed to get back to base.

In June, the squadron beat its record of number of sorties with 327, a figure that would not be surpassed before the transfer to the USAAF at the end of September. June was indeed busy. It started with three operations over France on the first day of the month (10.50, 12.50 and 17.50), but the Germans did not show up. Two more ops were carried out the next day and on the 3rd without incident. On the 4th, in the very early hours of the day, the squadron flew as air cover at 4000 feet for commandos making a raid on a RDF station inland of Plage-Ste-Cecile before withdrawing. Two Bf109s made an attempt to attack from behind, but the squadron turned into them and forced the German fighters to turn away. The following day, the squadron was back over Abbeville in France for a diversionary sweep with No. 72 Squadron. The Germans took off and engaged the Spitfires. The combat was rather balanced as the CO claimed one Fw190 as probably destroyed, but Californian P/O F. Hancock was posted missing. Up to the 20th, operational activity decreased owing mainly to bad weather. In this period of time, only three offensive ops were flown alongside some routine patrols. On the 20th, the squadron participated in another diversionary sweep over the Hardelot-Saint-Omer area while Bostons were bombing Le Havre. The Germans intercepted the squadron to their advantage, caught the last section of the formation and shot down P/O W.

No.133 (Eagle) Squadron in June 1942:
Standing, from left to right: P/O Leonard T. Ryerson from New Hampshire (killed 26.09.42), P/O George H. Middleton from Iowa (PoW 26.09.42), P/O Richard N. Beaty from New York, F/O Ervin L. Miller from Oklahoma, P/O Dick D. Gudmundsen from Idaho (killed 06.09.42), P/O Donald E. Lambert from California, P/O Dominic S. Gentile from Ohio, P/O J.M. Emerson (Intelligence Officer), F/O F.J.S. Chapman (Doctor), F/O D.G. Stavely-Dick (Adjutant), F/Sgt Grant E. Eichar from Iowa (killed 31.07.42), F/Sgt Chesley H. Robertson from Mississippi.
Front row, from left to right: P/O Carter W. Harp from Alabama (killed 31.07.42), P/O William A. Arends from North Dakota (killed 20.06.42), P/O Gilbert I. Omens from Illinois (killed 26.07.42), P/O Edwin D. Taylor from Oklahoma, F/L Coburn C. King from Missouri (killed 31.07.42), S/L Eric H. Thomas, F/L Donald J.M. Blakeslee from Ohio, P/O George B. Sperry from California (PoW 26.09.42), P/O Eric Doorly from New Jersey, P/O Karl K. Kimbro from Mississippi, P/O William H. Baker from Texas (killed 26.09.42).

BM260/MD-C was lost on 5 June 1942 with its pilot, P/O Hancock.

Arends from North Dakota. Another sweep to Dunkirk was conducted on the 23rd without incident and, on the 24th, eight aircraft were sent on a convoy patrol from 05.00 hours. Two aircraft scrambled at 06.55, over Rye and Dungeness, to 20,000 feet. Pilot Officers G.I. Omens, from Illinois, and W.C. Slade, from Texas, saw a He111 escorted by three Bf109s, but the Eagles were unable to intercept. Before the end of the month, the squadron participated in another two sweeps over France, but no incidents were reported. However, in the same period to time, some patrols were flown and on the 27th, while patrolling Tenterden at 28,000 feet, F/L D.L.M. Blakeslee, the new B Flight CO, and P/O C.W. Harp from Alabama saw a Ju88 flying below at 27,500 feet. They chased it back to Boulogne and although they fired all their cannon rounds, neither was able to get within 400 yards and no claim was filed. Later on, Blakeslee filed a report for a Ju88 damaged. On the last day of June, the squadron made a move to Lympne.

The first week of July was spent flying uneventful patrols. It was not until the 7th that the squadron returned to France when A Flight escorted Hurribombers over Fécamp in company with a flight from No. 234 Squadron. This was the only major action flown from Lympne and the unit returned to Biggin Hill a few days later. July 12 was a busy day with constant patrols flown between 05.10 and 09.15 before the squadron took part in a fighter sweep over the French coast around midday. Later that day it acted as escort cover, with the rest of the Wing, for Bostons bombing Abbeville aerodrome. More ops were flown over the Continent during the next few days, including the first mass Rhubarb, from 20 July. The end of July was approaching and, despite a lot of sorties, no combats were experienced to change the routine. Sadly, this routine was broken on the 28th when P/O B.P. deHaven from Kentucky was killed a flying accident. The reasons for the crash would never be clearly established. Eventually, what the Eagle pilots were looking for, dogfights with the Luftwaffe, occurred on the 31st during the day's first sweep over France early in the afternoon. They were escorting twelve Bostons targeting Abbeville aerodrome once more and 133 was flying with Nos. 65 and 72 Squadrons. The unit was acting as close escort to the Bostons, flying at 8000 feet, which bombed the aerodrome without incident. However, just before reaching the coast on the way back, a number of Fw190s appeared and a fierce melee ensued. Two confirmed victories were claimed in sequence by P/O W.H. Baker and P/O E.D. Taylor (Oklahoma), the latter also claiming a damaged Fw190. However, the squadron's casualties were not light. A Flight lost F/L C.C. King from Missouri, P/O C.W. Harp and F/Sgt G.E. Eichar (RCAF) from Iowa. All were shot down and killed. The same day, the squadron went to Gravesend where it remained before returning to Lympne on 17 August.

On 1 August, 133 flew its first operation from Gravesend, an escort for six Bostons bombing Bruges in Belgium. It was an uneventful way to start the month and all aircraft returned safely. Convoy patrols were flown over the next few days before the squadron was sent on an anti-shipping sweep off Boulogne and Le Havre on the 5th. No ships were seen. That day, temporary command was given to F/L Blakeslee as S/L Thomas had been promoted to Wing Commander and left to become wing leader of the Biggin Hill Wing. The next day, 133 participated in another sweep over the Belgian coast, escorting the 307th Fighter Squadron's (FS) Spitfires. An uneventful *Rodeo* was flown on the 9th and no further sorties were followed until the 15th. Having returned to Lympne, the squadron escorted twelve B-17 Flying Fortresses to Rouen, the first mission by these bombers over the European continent. On the 18th, with 65 Squadron and the USAAF's 307th FS, the unit flew another *Rodeo* to Dunkirk. They made a wide detour inland from Dunkirk and were just inland of Sangatte when they were attacked by about ten Fw190s. Led by F/L Blakeslee, the squadron made a 360 degree orbit, turning inside a couple of the Fw190s which allowed Blakeslee to give one a good burst. Plenty of cannon shells hit the enemy aircraft and the German pilot abandoned his fatally hit aircraft. The remaining enemy aircraft disappeared and no further combat took place. All of the Spitfires returned to base safely. On 19 August, Operation *Jubilee* was launched. The RAF had to play an important role in supporting the

Don Blakeslee about to taxi EN851/MD-U out for another op during the summer of 1942. He would make several claims while flying this aircraft.

William A. Arends, from North Dakota, just before he was shot down and killed by Fw190s on 20 June 1942. He had joined 133 Sqn the previous March. He's posing on the wing of his Spitfire, EP168.

various naval and army elements. As far as 133 Squadron was concerned, four patrols were carried out – 0720-0840, 1015-1130, 1225-1345 and 1955-2055. On the first patrol, led by Blakeslee, the squadron was tasked with orbiting over Dieppe at 7,000 feet shortly before 08.00. Soon after they arrived over the target, the enemy appeared. In the ensuing melee, Blakeslee and P/O W.H. Baker shot down one Fw190 each while F/Sgt R.L. Alexander from Illinois opened his score by claiming a probable Fw190. The squadron suffered no casualties. The second patrol also led to furious combats. This time, 133 was required to fly at 12,000 feet over Dieppe. Combat commenced immediately the target was reached. As the Americans turned for home, no less than two Fw190s, one Ju88, and one Do217 were claimed as destroyed, the victorious pilots being F/L E.G. Bretell, a British pilot recently posted in as a flight commander to replace F/L King (killed on 31 July), F/L Blakeslee, and P/O D.S. Gentile from Ohio who claimed the Ju88 and a Fw190. A number of other pilots also made claims: New Yorker P/O R.N. Beaty with a Do217 and a Fw190 damaged, F/L Blakeslee, P/O W.H. Baker and P/O G.G. Wright from Pennsylvania each claimed a Fw190 damaged, as well P/O D.D. Gudmunsden from Idaho, who was flying an American Spitfire (307th FS/MX-K), and P/O Doorly and Bretell also damaged a Do217 each. The harvest of claims was not over and during the third patrol, F/Sgt R.L. Alexander added a Do217 destroyed while F/L Blakeslee and F/O J.C. Nelson from Colorado claimed a damaged Fw190 and Do217 respectively. That was, without a doubt, the day of fame for the squadron as it made all of these claims without loss.

The next day, 133 carried out a *Rodeo* over Saint-Omer as a diversionary sweep. No combat was reported. That was the squadron's last operational use of the Spitfire Mk.V as it was detached to Martlesham for a course of air gunnery training and re-equipped with the Spitfire Mk.IX, but still continuing using a handful of Mk.Vs for training; one of them was lost during a practice flight on the 19th causing the death of his pilot, Pilot Officer S.M. Schatzberg from New York City. However, after debuting with the then rare and precious Mk.IX, the Spitfire Mk.Vs returned at the end of September in time for the unit's transfer to the USAAF where it became the 336th FS.

Claims - 133 Squadron (Confirmed and Probable)

Date	Pilot	SN	Origin	Type	Serial	Code	Nb	Cat.
05.02.42	F/L Hugh A.S. **JOHNSTONE**	RAF No. 88723	RAF	Do217	**P8195**		0.25	C*
	P/O Marion A. **JACKSON**	RAF No. 100519	(US)/RAF		**P9397**		0.25	C*
26.04.42	F/L Caroll W. **McCOLPIN**	RAF No. 61926	(US)/RAF	Fw190	**BM300**		1.0	C
27.04.42	P/O Robert L. **PEWITT**	RAF No. 100528	(US)/RAF	Fw190	**BL988**		1.0	P
	P/O William H. **BAKER**	RAF No. 108826	(US)/RAF	Fw190	**BL492**		1.0	P
17.05.42	P/O Moran S. **MORRIS**	RAF No. 102052	(US)/RAF	Bf109	**BL996**		1.0	P
	F/L Caroll W. **McCOLPIN**	RAF No. 61926	(US)/RAF	Bf109	**BM300**		1.0	C
	F/L Caroll W. **McCOLPIN**	RAF No. 61926	(US)/RAF	Bf109	**BM300**		1.0	P
19.05.42	P/O Moran S. **MORRIS**	RAF No. 105052	(US)/RAF	Bf109	**BL996**		1.0	C
	F/Sgt Carter W. **HARP**	CAN./ R.74201	(US)/RCAF	Bf109	**BL982**		2.0	C
05.06.42	S/L Eric H. **THOMAS**	RAF No. 39138	RAF	Bf109	**BM263**	MD-A	1.0	P
31.07.42	P/O William H. **BAKER**	RAF No. 108826	(US)/RAF	Fw190	**EN924**		1.0	C
	P/O Edwin D. **TAYLOR**	RAF No. 102053	(US)/RAF	Fw190	**BM591**		1.0	C
18.08.42	F/L Donald J.M. **BLAKESLEE**	CAN./ J.4551	(US)/RCAF	Bf109	**EN951**	MD-U	1.0	C

Date	Pilot		S/N	Origin	Serial	Code		Fate	
19.08.42	F/Sgt Richard L. **Alexander**	Can./ R.67881	(us)/RCAF	Fw190	**BL773**		1.0	P
	F/L Donald J.M. **Blakeslee**	Can./ J.4551	(us)/RCAF	Fw190	**EN951**	MD-U	1.0	P
	P/O William H. **Baker**	RAF No. 108826	(us)/RAF	Fw190	**EN834**		1.0	C
	F/L Edward G. **Bretell**	RAF No. 61053	RAF	Fw190	**AD237**		1.0	C
	F/L Donald J.M. **Blakeslee**	Can./ J.4551	(us)/RCAF	Do217	**EN951**	MD-U	1.0	C
	P/O Dominic S. **Gentile**	RAF No. 112302	(us)/RAF	Fw190	**BM530**		1.0	C
				Ju88	**BM530**		1.0	C
	F/Sgt Richard L. **Alexander**	Can./ R.67881	(us)/RCAF	Do217	**AB910**		1.0	C

Total: 21.5

*Shared with two No.253 Sqn pilots, P/O P. Landers and Sgt J.C. Tate.

Summary of the aircraft lost on Operations - 133 Squadron

Date	Pilot	S/N	Origin	Serial	Code	Fate
16.03.42	P/O Hugh C. **Brown**	RAF No. 103467	(us)/RAF	**X4353**		†
27.04.42	F/Sgt Walter C. **Wicker**	Can./ R.74415	(us)/RCAF	**BM264**		†
29.04.42	P/O Eric **Doorly**	RAF No. 101458	(us)/RAF	**BL995**	MD-G	-
19.05.42	P/O Robert L. **Pewitt**	RAF No. 100528	(us)/RAF	**BL988**		†
	P/O David R. **Florance**	Can./ J.15193	(us)/RCAF	**AD502**		†
31.05.42	P/O William K. **Ford**	RAF No. 111238	(us)/RAF	**BL961**		†
	P/O Moran S. **Morris**	RAF No. 102052	(us)/RAF	**BL996**		†
05.06.42	P/O Fletcher **Hancock**	RAF No. 112280	(us)/RAF	**BM260**	MD-C	†
20.06.42	P/O William A. **Arends**	RAF No. 112280	(us)/RAF	**EP168**		†
31.07.42	F/L Coburn C. **King**	RAF No. 100521	(us)/RAF	**BL938**		†
	P/O Carter W. **Harp**	Can./ J.15389	(us)/RCAF	**BL982**		†
	F/Sgt Grant E. **Eichar**	Can./ R.83097	(us)/RCAF	**BM646**		†

Total: 12

Summary of the aircraft lost by accident - 133 Squadron

Date	Pilot	S/N	Origin	Serial	Code	Fate
05.02.42	F/Sgt Frederick C. **Austin**	Can./ R.58580	(us)/RCAF	**W3379**		-
03.04.42	P/O Samuel F. **Whedon**	RAF No. 101462	(us)/RAF	**P8438**		†
	P/O William A. **Arends**	RAF No. 112280	(us)/RAF	**P8595**		-
25.04.42	Sgt Grant E. **Eichar**	Can./ R.83097	(us)/RCAF	**BL967**		-
28.07.42	P/O Ben P. **DeHaven**	RAF No. 116467	(us)/RAF	**BL807**		†
19.09.42	P/O Seymour M. **Schatzberg**	RAF No. 118585	(us)/RAF	**EP167**		†

Total: 6

IN MEMORIAM

Spitfire Mk V - The Eagle Squadrons

Name	Service No	Rank	Age	Origin	Date	Serial
ALLEN, Thomas Willcase	CAN./ J.15015	F/L	27	(US)/RCAF	31.05.42	W3645
ARENDS, William Albert	RAF No. 112280	P/O	24	(US)/RAF	20.06.42	EP168
ATKINSON, Roger Hall	RAF No. 102048	P/O	20	(US)/RAF	15.10.41	AD123
AUSTIN, Frederick Carlton	CAN./ R.58580	F/Sgt	n/k	(US)/RCAF	17.04.42	AD498
BODDING, Cral Olaf	RAF No. 108628	P/O	27	(US)/RAF	28.04.42	AD289
BROSSMER, Robert Vincent	RAF No. 106352	P/O	27	(US)/RAF	04.05.42	AD460
BROWN, Hugh Card	RAF No. 103467	P/O	21	(US)/RAF	16.03.42	X4353
CHATTERSON, Lawrence Albert	RAF No. 100987	P/O	24	(US)/RAF	22.10.41	AA759
DeHAVEN, Ben Perry	RAF No. 116467	P/O	25	(US)/RAF	28.07.42	BL807
EICHAR, Grant Eugene	CAN./ J.15650	P/O	27	(US)/RCAF	31.07.42	BM646
EVANS, Jack E.	CAN./ R.98138	F/Sgt	21	(US)/RCAF	27.08.42	AD196
FENLAW, Hillard Sidney	RAF No. 61924	P/O	24	(US)/RAF	07.09.41	AB900
FLORANCE, David Ray	CAN./ J.15193	P/O	22	(US)/RCAF	19.05.42	AD502
FLYNN, John Van Liew	RAF No. 61956	P/O	29	(US)/RAF	27.04.42	BM206
FORD, William Kenneth	RAF No. 111238	P/O	22	(US)/RAF	31.05.42	BL961
FREIBERG, Ralph William	RAF No. 110340	P/O	31	(US)/RAF	04.05.42	P8794
GILLILAND, Jack Dewberry	RAF No. 106510	P/O	22	(US)/RAF	08.01.42	W3240
HANCOCK, Fletcher	RAF No. 113991	P/O	22	(US)/RAF	05.06.42	BM260
HARP, Carter Woodruff	CAN./ J.15389	P/O	33	(US)/RCAF	31.07.42	BL982
HELSGASON, Joseph Field	RAF No. 114001	P/O	29	(US)/RAF	06.08.42	W3709
HOLDER, Kenneth LeRoy	RAF No. 118173	P/O	27	(US)/RAF	12.12.41	AA871
INABINET, William Burness	RAF No. 108637	P/O	22	(US)/RAF	09.01.42	AB783
KING, Coburn Clark	RAF No. 100521	F/L	33	(US)/RAF	31.07.42	BL938
MAYS, Ben Freeman	RAF No. 106509	P/O	28	(US)/RAF	12.04.42	AB810
McGERTY, Thomas Paul	RAF No. 61927	P/O	21	(US)/RAF	17.09.41	W3509
MEARES, Stanley Thomas	RAF No. 37683	S/L	25	RAF	15.11.41	W3963
MOONEY, John Joseph	CAN./ J.15024	F/L	21	(US)/RCAF	16.06.42	W3841
MORRIS, Moran Scott	RAF No. 102052	P/O	24	(US)/RAF	31.05.42	BL996
PATTERSON, Richard Fuller	CAN./ J.2928	P/O	26	(US)/RCAF	07.12.41	W3711
PEWITT, Robert Lewis	RAF No. 100528	P/O	22	(US)/RAF	19.05.42	BL988
SCARBOROUGH, Ross Orden	RAF No. 65976	P/O	19	(US)/RAF	15.11.41	W3627
SLATER, John Tassie*	RAF No. 116465	P/O	24	(US)/RAF	21.09.42	P8339
TAYLOR, James LaRue	RAF No. 110338	P/O	28	(US)/RAF	19.08.42	AD569
TAYLOR, William Douglas	RAF No. 115122	P/O	24	(US)/RAF	31.08.42	BM305
TEICHEIRA, George	RAF No. 114074	P/O	22	(US)/RAF	01.06.42	BM386
TOBIN, Eugene Quimby	RAF No. 81622	F/O	24	(US)/RAF	07.09.41	W3801
YOUNG, Norman Dudley	RAF No. 116163	P/O	26	(US)/RAF	31.07.42	AA732
WHEDON, Samuel Fisk	RAF No. 100531	P/O	21	(US)/RAF	03.04.42	P8438
WICKER, Walter Charles	CAN./ R.74415	F/Sgt	20	(US)/RCAF	27.04.42	BM264
ZAVAKOS, Frank George	RAF No. 108645	P/O	24	(US)/RAF	02.06.42	BM249

As per 121 ORB, but Slater is officially a USAAF loss as O-885133, having made his transfer on 16 September.

Total: 40

United Kingdom: 1, USA: 39

n/k: not known

Supermarine Spitfire Mk.VB AB875
No. 71 (Eagle) Squadron
Pilot Officer Joseph M. KELLY (USA)
Martlesham Heath (UK), February 1942

Supermarine Spitfire Mk.VB BL287
No. 71 (Eagle) Squadron
Pilot Officer Leo S. NOMIS (USA)
Martlesham Heath (UK), March 1942

Supermarine Spitfire Mk.VB W3711
No. 121 (Eagle) Squadron
Pilot Officer Richard F. PATTERSON (USA)
Kirton-in-Lindsey (UK), December 1941

Supermarine Spitfire Mk.VB BM581
No. 121 (Eagle) Squadron
Pilot Officer William P. KELLY (USA)
Southend (UK), July 1942

Supermarine Spitfire Mk.VB EN951
No. 133 (Eagle) Squadron
Flight Lieutenant Donald J.M. BLAKESLEE (USA)
Gravesend (UK), August 1942

Supermarine Spitfire Mk.VB BM263
No. 133 (Eagle) Squadron
Squadron Leader Eric H. THOMAS
Kirton-in-Lindsey (UK), Spring 1942

Supermarine Spitfire Mk.VB BM263
No. 133 (Eagle) Squadron
Squadron Leader Eric H. THOMAS
Kirton-in-Lindsey (UK), Spring 1942

SQUADRONS! - The series

The Supermarine
SPITFIRE Mk. VI
No.1

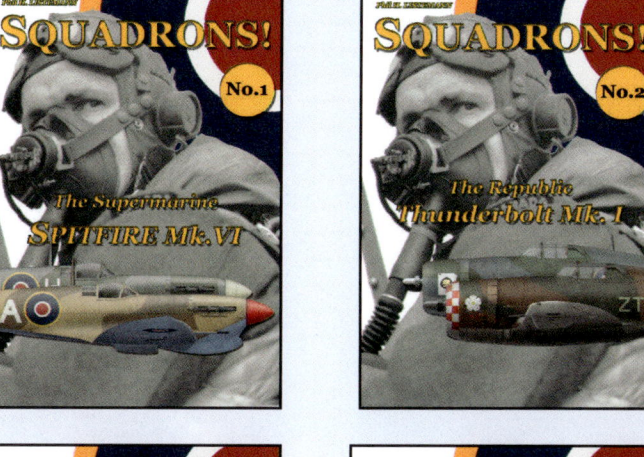

The Republic
Thunderbolt Mk. I
No.2

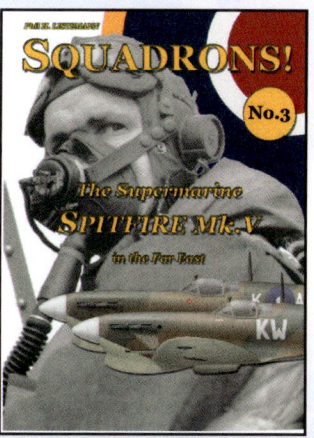

The Supermarine
SPITFIRE Mk. V
in the Far East
No.3

The Boeing
Fortress Mk.1
No.4

The Supermarine
SPITFIRE Mk. XII
No.5

The Supermarine
SPITFIRE Mk. VII
No.6

The Supermarine
SPITFIRE F.21
No.7

The Handley Page
Halifax Mk.1
No.8

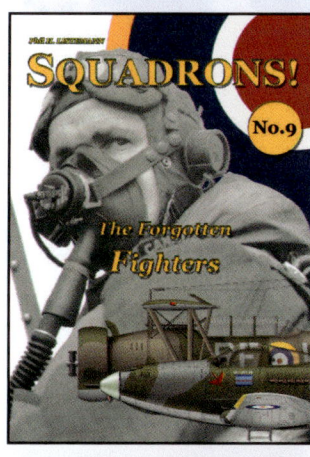

The Forgotten
Fighters
No.9

The North American
Mustang Mk. IV
in Western Europe
No.10

The North American
Mustang Mk. IV
over Italy and the Balkans
No.11

The Supermarine
Spitfire Mk. XVI
- The British -
No.12

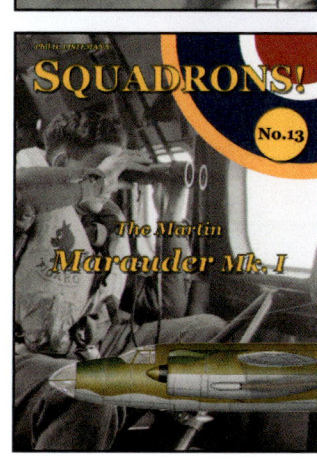

The Martin
Marauder Mk. I
No.13

The Supermarine
Spitfire Mk. VIII
in the southwest Pacific - The British
No.14

The Gloster
Meteor F. I & F. III
No.15

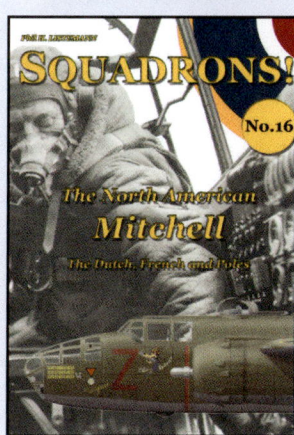

The North American
Mitchell
The Dutch, French and Poles
No.16

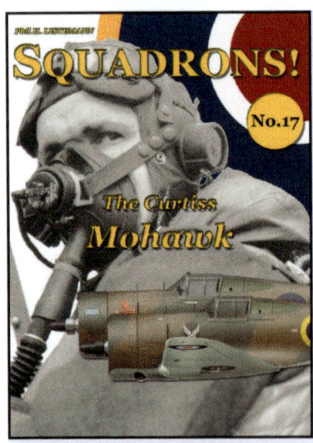

SQUADRONS! No.17

The Curtiss
Mohawk

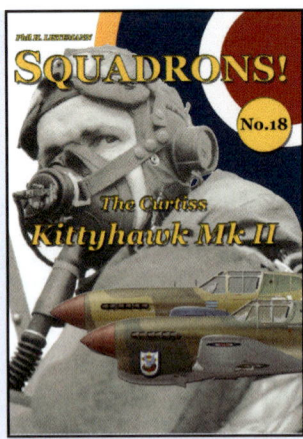

SQUADRONS! No.18

The Curtiss
Kittyhawk Mk II

SQUADRONS! No.19

The Boulton Paul
Defiant

Day and Night fighter

SQUADRONS! No.20

The Supermarine
Spitfire Mk. VIII

in the Southwest Pacific - The Australians -

SQUADRONS! No.21

The Boeing
Fortress Mk. II & Mk. III

SQUADRONS! No.22

The Douglas
Boston & Havoc

- The Australians -

SQUADRONS! No.23

The Republic
Thunderbolt Mk. II

SQUADRONS! No.24

The Douglas
Boston & Havoc

- Night Fighter -

SQUADRONS! No.25

The Supermarine
SPITFIRE Mk. V

- The Eagle Squadrons -

SQUADRONS!
No.3

FIGHTER LEADERS
of the RAF, RAAF, RCAF, RNZAF & SAAF in WW2
Volume I
Phil H. Listemann

Fighter Leaders
RAAF, RCAF, RNZAF & SAAF in WW2
Volume III
Phil H. Listemann

USN AIRCRAFT
1922-1962
G-228
Vol.4:
Type Designation Letters
'BF', 'BT' & 'F' (Pt-1)

RAF, DOMINION & ALLIED SQUADRON
AT WAR:
STUDY, HISTORY AND STATISTICS

No.137 Squadron
1941 - 1945

COMPILED BY
PHIL H. LISTEMANN
WITH
CHRIS THOMAS

SQUADRONS!
No.10
The North American
Mustang Mk. IV
in Western Europe

www.RAF-IN-COMBAT.com

- USN Aircraft 1922-1962 -
- Squadrons! -
- RAF, Dominion and Allied squadrons at War -
- Allied Wings -
- Famous squadrons of WW2 -
- Fighter Leaders -

RAF, DOMINION & ALLIED SQUADRON
AT WAR:
STUDY, HISTORY AND STATISTICS

No.131 (County of Kent) Squadron
1941 - 1945

Famous Commonwealth Squadrons of WW2
No.453 (R.A.A.F.) Squadron
1941-1945
Buffalo, Spitfire

ALLIED WINGS

ALLIED WINGS

Printed in Great Britain
by Amazon